T0178741

I thank God for *Aging Faithfully*. It is a book for you regardless of your age, for the truth of the matter is, we are all aging . . . every single one of us. Alice Fryling lovingly leads us through the ups and downs, the losses and the treasures we experience in the interior chambers of our soul throughout our aging. I recommend Alice Fryling as a reliable and faithful guide through this multifaceted adventure of aging.

    RICHARD J. FOSTER, author of *Celebration of Discipline* and *Sanctuary of the Soul*

This lovely book is full of wisdom, encouragement, and hard-won insights from one who knows whereof she speaks. And questions . . . the questions alone are worth the price of the book, helping us enter the depths of what God has for us in this stage of our human journey! The bad news is that we all need this book or will need it eventually. The good news is that with Alice as our companion, we can experience aging as a season rich with holy invitations from God leading to immense satisfaction, if we can stop resisting those invitations and just say yes!

    RUTH HALEY BARTON, founder of Transforming Center, author of *Sacred Rhythms*

Age alone does not equal spiritual, emotional, or relational maturity. Our world is filled with adolescent, false-self, immature older adults who need the biblical wisdom, relational maturity, and graced fortitude of Alice Fryling. By prayerfully embracing our holy losses, hidden in the cross of Christ, we are ready to receive our holy invitations, advancing the Kingdom of heaven. The end-of-chapter reflections and the rich appendices are icing on this delicious piece of literary cake. Thank you, Alice!

STEPHEN A. MACCHIA, founder and president of Leadership Transformations

Getting older is one of life's journeys few of us sign up for but all of us must take. In *Aging Faithfully*, Alice Fryling draws from her decades of experience as a wise spiritual guide to equip us for this holy adventure. Reading Alice's book brought me closer to the truth that God has given me everything I need to age not only faithfully but joyfully.

PEGGY WEHMEYER, former ABC News correspondent, grandmother of five

As we move into our sixties and beyond, we experience a profound silence. The voices of our mentors are gone. Those from whom we received direction and encouragement are silenced at a time when we need their help the most. *Aging Faithfully* speaks directly into that silent space. For those of us who long to live faithfully into maturity, this book provides direction, new possibilities, and needed encouragement. These are meant to be the most fruitful years of our lives!

MICHAEL CARD, musician, author, teacher

Alice Fryling has uncovered the secrets as to why some grow older with grace and joy while others are defeated by the inevitable losses. Her wisdom brings hope and laughter! She quotes Psalm 92, which tells how the righteous can still bear fruit in old age and be "always green and full of sap"! This isn't just a book for the elderly; it's also for those who love them.

DEE BRESTIN, author of *Falling in Love with Jesus* and *He Calls You Beautiful*

In this age-denying culture, thank God for Alice Fryling! She is a wise, warm, honest, and companionable guide who shows us that the "liminal space" of aging can bring unexpected growth and freedoms. Page by page, she gently corrects our nearsightedness, replacing it with beautiful, biblical ways to become "more fruitful" even as we become "less productive." As the years pass, I know I will reach for this book again and again.

LESLIE LEYLAND FIELDS, editor of *The Wonder Years: Forty Women Over Forty on Aging, Faith, Beauty, and Strength*

Today, over ten thousand people in the United States will turn sixty-five. Very few are prepared for what lies ahead, both the incredible opportunities and the inevitable losses. Alice Fryling, in *Aging Faithfully*, is a wise and vulnerable guide who invites us to join her on a journey into deeper meaning and truer flourishing. This is an excellent book for people in the third third of life and for those who love them.

MARK D. ROBERTS, PhD, senior strategist, Max De Pree Center for Leadership at Fuller Seminary

The apostle Paul tells us in 1 Corinthians 13:12 that we can see eternity as though we're looking at it through a dim mirror. The final movement of our lives carries with it the opportunity to move closer to that mirror, where the light and shadows of old age present to us an image of God, ourselves, and others that we've not been able to fully behold at earlier stages of our lives. Alice Fryling's gentle, honest writing illumines the losses, questions, fears, and longings we carry with us into the aging process. *Aging Faithfully* is a trustworthy guide to the light and shadows of our final stage of life on earth with honesty, offering us a gracious and hopeful sense of the welcome that awaits us on the other side of that dim mirror.

MICHELLE VAN LOON, author of *Becoming Sage: Cultivating Meaning, Purpose, and Spirituality in Midlife*

In *Aging Faithfully: The Holy Invitation of Growing Older*,
Alice Fryling takes the reader on a journey from a frank
look at the losses that accompany aging to hope and
purpose in our later years. The processing questions at
the end of each chapter will be valuable to anyone as they
anticipate or experience the losses and joys of those years.

JOE BERNARDY, director of Navigators Encore

I have been waiting for such a book as this because even
as our bodies age, our desire for a life with meaning and
connections does not. Fryling invites us to embrace all
the wonder and possibilities of each day in communion
with our changing bodies. With wit and grace wedded to
unadorned realities, Fryling spiritually guides us to the gift
of growing old in and with Christ. She closes the book
with spiritual wisdom for finding peace in uselessness,
loneliness, brokenness, and our last season, and I found
myself weeping. This book touches the soul for those of us
who want to flourish and not wither till our final breath is
given up. Thank you, Alice, for your faithfulness.

MARYKATE MORSE, author, executive dean of Portland
Seminary

Aging Faithfully provides a road map for trusting and
growing in Christ through the changing seasons of

our lives. Alice Fryling encourages her readers through Scripture, stories, and personal anecdotes. She provides dedicated space for reflection and meditation where readers can record their own thoughts in response to her writing prompts. It is a beautiful book; I recommend it.

SHIRLEY V. HOOGSTRA, JD, president of Council for Christian Colleges & Universities

You know you're reading an excellent book when you have your highlighter out, marking numerous passages for further reflection, while at the same time jotting down names of friends who will benefit as well. *Aging Faithfully* is just such a resource. With tempered wisdom, empathy, and the navigational skills of a seasoned spiritual director, Alice Fryling takes us through the liminal space that is the aging process, helping readers reframe elderhood as a new stage to anticipate growth and fruitfulness.

MAGGIE WALLEM ROWE, author of *This Life We Share*

Wow. After reading the book, I began to realize, for the first time, that aging is part of God's plan for me. As I embrace that, I see that there are treasures, invitations, and blessings ahead that I did not expect.

MICHAEL A. WHITNEY, senior pastor of First Baptist Church, Freeport, Maine

AGING
FAITHFULLY

The Holy Invitation of Growing Older

ALICE FRYLING

NavPress

A NavPress resource published in alliance
with Tyndale House Publishers

NavPress is the publishing ministry of The Navigators, an international Christian organization and leader in personal spiritual development. NavPress is committed to helping people grow spiritually and enjoy lives of meaning and hope through personal and group resources that are biblically rooted, culturally relevant, and highly practical.

For more information, visit NavPress.com.

Aging Faithfully: The Holy Invitation of Growing Older

Copyright © 2021 by Alice Fryling. All rights reserved.

A NavPress resource published in alliance with Tyndale House Publishers

NAVPRESS and the NavPress logo are registered trademarks of NavPress, The Navigators, Colorado Springs, CO. *TYNDALE* is a registered trademark of Tyndale House Ministries. Absence of ® in connection with marks of NavPress or other parties does not indicate an absence of registration of those marks.

The Team:
David Zimmerman, Acquisitions Editor; Elizabeth Schroll, Copy Editor; Olivia Eldredge, Operations Manager; Nicole Grimes, Cover Designer; Julie Chen, Interior Designer

Cover images are the property of their respective copyright holders, and all rights are reserved. Roots © enterphoto/Adobe Stock; tree growth © Production Perig/Adobe Stock; mature tree © LiliGraphie/Adobe Stock; citrus leaves © New Africa/Depositphotos; leaf close-up © Dan Hodgkins/Unsplash. Author photograph copyright © 2021 by Jennifer Blazis and used with permission. Interior photograph of Alice Fryling with her grandmother by Willard Watts, 1946 and used with permission.

All Scripture quotations, unless otherwise indicated, are taken from the Holy Bible, *New International Version,*® *NIV.*® Copyright © 1973, 1978, 1984, 2011 by Biblica, Inc.® Used by permission. All rights reserved worldwide. Scripture quotations marked KJV are taken from the *Holy Bible*, King James Version. Scripture quotations marked MSG are taken from *The Message*, copyright © 1993, 2002, 2018 by Eugene H. Peterson. Used by permission of NavPress. All rights reserved. Represented by Tyndale House Publishers. Scripture quotations marked NIrV are taken from the Holy Bible, *New International Reader's Version,*® *NIrV.*® Copyright © 1995, 1996, 1998, 2014 by Biblical, Inc.® Used by permission. All rights reserved worldwide. Scripture quotations marked NRSV are taken from the New Revised Standard Version Bible, copyright © 1989, Division of Christian Education of the National Council of the Churches of Christ in the United States of America. Used by permission. All rights reserved. Scripture quotations marked RSV are taken from the Revised Standard Version of the Bible, copyright © 1946, 1952, and 1971 National Council of the Churches of Christ in the United States of America. Used by permission. All rights reserved.

Some of the anecdotal illustrations in this book are true to life and are included with the permission of the persons involved. All other illustrations are composites of real situations, and any resemblance to people living or dead is purely coincidental.

Content from personal interviews is based on anonymous email submissions requested by the author.

For information about special discounts for bulk purchases, please contact Tyndale House Publishers at csresponse@tyndale.com, or call 1-855-277-9400.

ISBN 978-1-64158-359-6

Printed in China

27   26   25   24   23
7   6   5   4

To Bob—

Grow old along with me!

The best is yet to be,

The last of life, for which the first was made.

ROBERT BROWNING

Contents

Foreword

WHEN ALICE FRYLING asked if I might write the fore-word for this book, my immediate reaction was: yes, of course! I have admired and appreciated her writings and wisdom across the years, and I knew others felt the same and would surely profit from *Aging Faithfully*.

Then, as I began to read, I realized that I needed to read this book for myself, and not just to write a fore-word. I needed it for my own soul!

I am old enough to track with the challenges that come with aging. I don't need to be convinced they are real. I am moving near to the time when I will turn over the leadership of our mentoring ministry to our son, Kevin, and his colleagues. So I understand very personally what Alice writes about the anxiety that comes with losses and letting go.

The need to understand how aging is part of God's good plan is likewise very real to me. And the core message of this book is just that: God has a purpose in and for our aging. That purpose has to do with the hidden life of the Spirit so that, as the body grows older, our spirit may grow deeper and stronger. Our ongoing calling, in later years as in earlier years, is to die daily, perhaps even hourly, with our Lord, and to realize (especially in our later years) the reality and power of his death and of his resurrection.

This is a hard but crucial message to learn, and I appreciate how honestly Alice lets us know how she and her husband, Bob, keep learning.

As I prepared to write this foreword, I called Alice at her home in Colorado to ask what she hoped would speak to her readers, based on her own experience. She hesitated a moment, then said, "At my age, I want to be helpful and do more, but I just don't have the physical energy to do all I used to do and still want to do."

And then she added simply, "I need to trust that while there may be less of me, there will be more of Christ."

Around the same time, I asked my wife, Jeanie, to read the chapter on loss to get a taste for the book. When she finished reading, she looked up and said, "She's writing about me!" It is my hope and prayer that you, dear reader, and many others will also read and say, "She's writing about me—and she helps!"

Leighton Ford
founding president, Leighton Ford Ministries
Charlotte, North Carolina

Introduction

I HAVE CELEBRATED a lot of birthdays. Some of them were memorable. Some not so much. But long gone are the beautiful little-girl birthday cakes from my father's restaurant. Long gone are the party games in the backyard. I don't remember the names of my friends who came to the parties, but I do remember (heaven forbid!) the watermelon-seed-spitting contests we held. In those days, I thought I would forever love watermelon slices with big seeds and roses made of cake icing. It never occurred to me that I would change.

But I did change. Every year, I got older. I grew up from a little girl in a party dress to a young woman in professional clothes. Then, without even realizing what was happening, I became a middle-aged woman. I was married and had children. I supervised playdates, went to parent-teacher conferences, and navigated a calendar full of activities, my own and my children's. Before I saw it coming, I was sixty. When I turned sixty, my friends assured me that "Sixty is the new forty." I did not need to worry. I could still live as though I were forty. But deep inside, I knew that wasn't true. When I was forty, I had children at home, a husband at work, a smaller waistline, and more energy. When I turned sixty, my children had left home, my husband was thinking of retiring, and my life began to look very different. I began to ask, *Who in the world am I now? Who do I want to be?*

Looking back, I can see who I was as a little girl. I recognize myself as a wife, a mother, and a professional person. I know my Enneagram space and my Myers-Briggs letters. But I do not know who I am (or who I will be) as an older person. This is a little scary. I like knowing who I am. I do *not* like not knowing the future. Like the ancient sailors with their antique (and inaccurate) maps, I do not know where I am going.

So I set out to try to learn from others what the

terrain looks like. I began to check out books about aging from the library. I talked with friends and friends of friends. The advice I heard from books and friends was confusing. Some people told me all would be well. After all, they could still play tennis. Since I didn't play tennis when I was forty, let alone sixty, that didn't help. Others told me not to worry. They could still tie their own shoes at ninety. I hope I can do that, but I also hope for much more. Apparently, all of us experience the aging process differently, in light of our own life experiences.

Complicating things further was my sense that the aging process looks different at different ages. In our fifties, "old age" seems theoretical, something to deal with when the time comes. In our sixties, we begin noticing physical changes and experiencing losses in life that, for many, become wake-up calls on the journey to old age. For some, this reminds us that we need to begin to prepare for the journey of aging. For others, these changes and losses become places of resistance and denial. Rather than "giving in," some people do all they can to look young, act young, or convince others that they are young.

By the time we reach our seventies, the evidence of aging is usually more obvious. Our bodies and our energy levels begin to shout, "Would you please slow down?!" We may respond, "I can't!" Or, perhaps we shout back, "I don't want to!" By our eighties, my friends tell me, we no longer have the option to ignore what our bodies are saying to us.

Whatever our decade of life, we are never not aging. Our senior years usually include reflections of events that happened in small or large doses throughout our life. Now, in our senior years, we have the responsibility (or opportunity) to practice all that we have learned. But I needed help to learn how to do this. I needed someone to tell me more about how to experience my senior years in life-giving ways.

And so I began to look for perspectives that would help me embrace this mysterious human experience as a spiritual process. Rabbi Zalman Schachter-Shalomi wrote that "if we viewed elderhood as the crowning achievement of our lives, we would open the door with reverence and anticipation. Prayerfully, we would say, 'Oh my soul, you are growing something special and good inside me. How can I give it the proper sunshine and nourishment to ensure that it grows to health and vigor?'"[1] This perspective spoke to the longing of my heart as I looked for guidance in my new season of life. I longed to understand the uniqueness, the complexities, the needs, and the potential of my soul as I moved into old age.

I decided to make a list of questions many of us have about the spiritual dimension of aging. My preliminary list includes:

- Will aging change who we are?
- Will aging diminish us?
- How will aging change our relationships with family and friends?
- How will aging change our relationship with God?
- How will we respond to our aging bodies?
- What do we do about the things we do not like in this experience?
- Is there anything we do like about getting old?

In short, how can we prepare for this unknown, uniquely personal experience? In particular, what happens in our souls as we age?

On the wall of my study are some ancient maps. They are, notably, incomplete, much like the map for the rest of our lives. What if we set out, like so many of the explorers, and find a new land that wasn't supposed to be there? Perhaps, by God's grace, we will discover something good we never expected. Perhaps, by God's grace, it will be a land where we can continue to grow. I am coming to believe that old age will indeed be a place where I can experience God's love in ever deepening ways.

Thank you for joining me on the journey!

A DIFFERENT KIND
OF RETIREMENT

WHEN MY HUSBAND RETIRED a few years ago, I pictured myself sitting in the Howdy Doody Peanut Gallery, watching as the events unfolded. (Yes, I grew up watching *Howdy Doody*—on our black-and-white television.) Now I watched from the Gallery as Bob went through the difficult discernment process about the timing of his retirement. Then I watched as he grieved the loss of daily contact with colleagues and the personal validation that his job responsibilities gave to him. I watched him throw away the notes from hundreds of talks he would never give again. I watched as he faced his fear that the only excitement in the future might be on the golf course. The view from my Peanut Gallery was not Howdy Doody happy.

But I thought I didn't need to worry about retirement for myself. Because I had no regular job to retire from, I told myself that I was not retiring. I was a mother, an author, and a spiritual director—all jobs that would change as I aged but not through traditional retirement. I thought I was all set to go.

Only I wasn't. All of us, as we age, retire. We retire not just from jobs but from relationships, ways of thinking, and how we think about ourselves. We move on. We no longer find validation in activities and tasks that have been important to us for decades. We can no longer do the things we used to do. The next generation is doing those things better than we can. To become older, then, means we retire, whether we're getting paid for our work or not.

Retirement, whatever form it takes, is often our first step through the door with a sign above it: "Old Age Straight Ahead." If we notice the sign, we may cringe. We probably think we can handle retirement. But old age? Most of us don't even like the term, let alone what it means for us. Who put that sign there, and what does it mean?

For some, the step through the door is a defined moment: the transition away from employment, learning to live in the empty nest, an unexpected illness, the death of a parent, or the loss of a spouse. Others of us recognize the door only as we look back. We realize that gradual losses have built up in recent years, family dynamics have changed, and we are not getting as many calls for professional input. Whether the step through the door is clear or not, it is always a step into liminal space.

STEPPING INTO MYSTERY

"Liminal space" is the unknown place between where we are and where we will be. It is a place that is mysterious, vague, exciting, and scary, all wrapped up into something new and unformed. It is moving to where we have never been before.

The Old Testament book of Exodus describes the Israelites in liminal space as they left their familiar, if stressful, life in Egypt to follow Moses into a new land. Never mind that God said this was "a good and spacious land, a land flowing with milk and honey" (Exodus 3:8). The Israelites responded as most of us do when we enter an unknown season of life. When they ran into trouble, they complained, whined, and resisted: "Was it because there were no graves in Egypt that you brought us to the desert to die?" (Exodus 14:11). As we move from the familiar stresses of midlife to the unknown stresses of the aging process we, too, may object, resist, and complain. God might lead us by a long, circuitous route, as he did the Israelites. Perhaps, by God's grace, we might come to a promised land. But first, we need to go through liminal space.

And we all respond differently to walking into that liminal space. My friend George is a high-energy person. His first question in retirement was, *Now what exciting things can I do?* Other friends are paralyzed by retirement. What will I do now? Who am I now that I do not have a job description? Where is my family now that I need them? These questions do not have quick or easy answers, especially if we are looking for answers that have a spiritual perspective.

BLOSSOMING TREES

As my husband and I entered retirement and our senior years, one of the places we found perspective was in looking at the flowering pear tree outside Bob's study window. It had always been the last tree in the yard to shed its leaves in the fall, but the year he retired, the leaves stayed on the tree until February. As we looked at the tree, we wondered if those leaves were a symbol of all the dead leaves Bob was trying to release in his own life. When the leaves finally fell off the tree and the branches were bare, Bob's soul also felt bare. Then, in the spring, the tree blossomed. It was beautiful. When the blossoms were replaced with green leaves, the tree became a symbol of hope for both of us. We saw the glory of God in the rebirth of our pear tree. David, the Old Testament writer of many of the Psalms, made a similar observation about God's glory manifested all around us:

The heavens are telling the glory of God;
    and the firmament proclaims his handiwork.
Day to day pours forth speech,
    and night to night declares knowledge.
There is no speech, nor are there words;
    their voice is not heard;
yet their voice goes out through all the earth,
    and their words to the end of the world.

PSALM 19:1-4, NRSV

It was as though God was revealing something to us through our pear tree. Without the benefit of words, the Holy Spirit seemed to remind us that it was time to shed the past and wait for the green leaves of the future.

Our pear tree, then, gave a hint of how God might help us navigate this liminal space—through an image. In fact, God often uses images to explain truths to us. Sometimes we can understand unseen truths from things we can actually see. The Psalms made use of poetic images. The Old Testament prophets made use of instructive images. Jesus, the Master Storyteller, used analogies to describe how God works. The Kingdom of God, Jesus said in his parables, is like a farmer sowing seeds (Matthew 13:24-30), like a woman who finds a lost coin (Luke 15:8-10), and like a pearl buried in a field (Matthew 13:45-46).

GREEN AND FULL OF SAP

One of the Psalms describes, with an image, what our old age might look like. The psalmist observed,

> The righteous flourish like the palm tree,
>   and grow like a cedar in Lebanon.

> They are planted in the house of the LORD;
>> they flourish in the courts of our God.
> In old age they still produce fruit;
>> they are always green and full of sap.

PSALM 92:12-14, NRSV

The first time I read that description of old age I was young, and I laughed! Old people are saps indeed.

But there is another definition of sap—the one the psalmist meant. Sap is a fluid that gives the plant life and energy. God invites us to flourish in our senior years, knowing that we are still producing sap, and that this sap will still produce fruit in our lives, for the sake of others. As we grow into the senior season of life, we will be called on to make choices about how to nourish the trees that we are becoming. To keep the sap running, we will be invited to "choose life."

When the Israelites entered the last part of their journey out of Egypt (and into liminal space), God said to them through Moses, "I have set before you life and death. . . . Now choose life" (Deuteronomy 30:19). As I age, some days it feels easier than others to choose God's life-giving ways. Some days, I am content with the changes that aging brings. Other days, I complain and resist. On the more difficult days, I remember something else God said through Moses: "Now what I am commanding you today is not too difficult for you or beyond your reach. . . . No, the word is very near you; it is in your mouth and in your heart so you may obey it" (Deuteronomy 30:11, 14). In other words, I can do this. I can be the older person God has designed me to be. His Word will guide me. His Word is in my mouth and my heart. This is comforting and reassuring. New life in old age is not beyond our reach. God's Word lives in us and will guide us each day for the rest of our lives.

But learning to choose life means that I have much to *unlearn.* I have lived with many perspectives about life and myself that are simply not life-giving. I want to unlearn my compulsive belief that I need to earn God's love. I want to unlearn my belief that I am responsible to meet everyone's needs. I hope someday to unlearn my persistent belief that I must impress God, myself, or other people with who I am and what I do. I want to unlearn the value I place on productivity, busyness, and constant activity.

Unlearning these things is countercultural and counterintuitive. Yesterday someone greeted me with

"Hi, Alice! You keeping busy?" (How in the world do I answer THAT?!) This morning as I read our church newsletter, I was sad because there were so many activities I can no longer do. Things I used to engage in regularly no longer look the same to me. They are either too late in the night or too early in the morning. *Or, perhaps*, I mused to myself, *I just no longer want to do all those things.*

Listen! the Spirit whispers, *Perhaps God is creating something new in you to help you be green and full of sap even in your old age.* Perhaps I am changing. Perhaps God is freeing me from attitudes that have enslaved me in the past. When I complain that I run out of energy before I run out of day, I sense God smiling at me and whispering in the Holy Spirit's silent way, *Don't worry. It's okay. I love you even when you can't do all you used to do. I understand that and I will keep reminding you of my love.*

FRUITFULNESS OR PRODUCTIVITY

Another thing the Spirit reminds me, in the process of choosing life as I grow older, is that in this season, I can celebrate being more fruitful, even as I become less productive. Up until now, I have validated my life by

9

the tasks I get done and the accomplishments I achieve. In other words, for better or for worse, I have focused on my productivity. Now, God is inviting me to focus more on fruitfulness in my life.

There is a difference between productivity and fruitfulness. Productivity results from all the tasks I accomplish. Fruitfulness comes from within and includes nontangible ways I relate to others. I needed to be productive earlier in life as I worked hard in many ways to care for my family. The problem wasn't that I was being productive but my compulsive need to be "perfectly productive," preferably on my carefully worked-out time schedule. Now that I am invited to focus more on fruitfulness, my attitude is changing. The fruit of the Holy Spirit is "love, joy, peace, forbearance, kindness, goodness, faithfulness, gentleness and self-control" (Galatians 5:22-23). We do not make these things happen in our lives; God does. And it takes a long time. Being fruitful is more out of our control than being productive. As we age, we may find that we are not able to do as many tasks, but by the grace of God, we may find that there is more fruit in our lives than ever before.

I am thankful for the people who shared their fruitfulness with me when I was young. I think of my grandma, who paid attention to me and welcomed me into a place of love (a place that smelled like chocolate-chip cookies). I think of my Sunday-school teacher, who taught me that God loved me (and gave me prizes for memorizing Scripture verses). I think of the woman who led me in Bible studies in my college dorm room. And I think of my first supervisor when I entered campus ministry, who listened to me for hours over coffee and ice cream. I realize now that many of these people were not as "old" as I thought they were at the time, but as they listened to me and loved me, I experienced God's love, God's patience, his kindness, and his goodness. These "older" people did not rush on to the next item on their agenda. Their focused attention enriched my life. And now I find myself thinking of them, as God is inviting me to be more fruitful at a time when I cannot be as productive as I used to be. I hope that as I age, I will become more and more like those people who loved the younger me.

This shift from productivity to fruitfulness is liminal space for me. But it does not escape my notice that my adolescent granddaughter is also in liminal space. For her, it is the space between childhood and adulthood. For me, it is the space between the productivity of midlife and my unknown senior years. My granddaughter and I are going through liminal space together. From my vantage point, the relationship I have with my granddaughter is more fruitful than productive. I am more invested in loving her, listening to her, and supporting her than I am in teaching her all I know and that I want her to learn. I hope I see her through the eyes of our heavenly Father.

Fruitfulness is a slow and mysterious process. I cannot do the many things I might have done in years past, but by the grace of God, I have the mental and emotional capacity to love my granddaughter in ways I couldn't have in my busy, driven younger years. Some of the leaves on my tree have died but the sap is still running, the tree is still fruitful, and I am grateful.

SAVING THE BEST FOR LAST

Another image that encourages me as I live out the retirement years is the image of wine. When Jesus miraculously turned water into wine at the wedding feast, the steward at the wedding commented to the bridegroom, "Everyone serves the good wine first, and then the inferior wine after the guests have become drunk. But you have kept the good wine until now" (John 2:10, NRSV).

Using this as a metaphor for the aging process, I might say, "I thought you gave me the best gifts when I was young and able to use them well. I thought you would save the inferior gifts for when I am old and slow and nobody cares." Perhaps Jesus would answer me, "I have saved the best for the end of the party."

Wine is a good image for old age because wine comes from fermented fruit. Fermentation is the process by which grapes transform into wine. The science of fermentation is called "zymology." Spiritually speaking, it is not too far-fetched to say that as we age, God is performing a zymological act to ferment us into new wine. It takes a long time for grapes to ferment into wine. Perhaps that is why God saves the best wine for the end of our lives. We need time to ferment.

My friends who are wine connoisseurs describe wine by its flavor, the kind of wood barrel where it was fermented, and the meals it should be served with. I often laugh at the descriptions of the wines on a dinner menu. I don't know what they are talking about! But I do know that we need to pay attention to the wine of our own lives. What is fermenting in our lives? What are the fruits—not the accomplishments—that we can focus on now? What foods (activities) will "pair" well with our lives in this season? Like experienced wine tasters, we can begin noticing whatever God is creating in us and for us in this season of our lives.

NEW WINESKINS

On another occasion, Jesus used a different image of wine to describe our spiritual journey. In a discussion about fasting with his disciples, Jesus said, "No one pours new wine into old wineskins. Otherwise, the new wine will burst the skins. . . . New wine must be poured into new wineskins" (Luke 5:37-38). Commentators tell us that Jesus was referring to how wineskins (made from animal skins) stretched with use. If new wine was poured into old skins, it might expand as it continued fermenting, and the skins could break.[1]

This image, too, can be applied to the process of aging. As God graciously continues to ferment the fruits of the Spirit in our lives into new wine, he pours this wine into the wineskins of our souls. Our bodies may become old as we age, but the wineskins of our souls need to continually be made new. If our wineskins are old, they may not be able to hold the new wine. It is significant that Jesus taught about the importance of new wineskins when he was responding to questions about the rules for fasting. The Pharisees were used to a life of obeying the law and wanted to know what the rules were. Jesus wanted to describe new wineskins, full of grace and love.

Many of us arrive at the door of old age with a lot of rules, which have become laws for ourselves and for others. Our old wineskins probably have held a lot of these laws. Some of these rules are self-made. Some we have been taught. Most of our rules look very good. But Jesus came to replace a legalistic perspective with grace. As we age, God creates new wineskins in our souls to contain our new attitudes toward life. We may find that we are able to hold life more loosely. The things we thought were so important seem less so. When we grow older, we may (hopefully) become more flexible and less rigid toward ourselves and toward others. Our new wineskins become places in our souls to contain the transformations God offers us as we age. As we receive these new wineskins for our well-fermented wine, we will grow in our capacity to love others well.

The images of trees and wine God gives in Scripture give glimpses of how different our retirement years might be. They invite us to look for new life in the ongoing changes age brings. As we let go of youthful perspectives we have outgrown, we become people who are like finely aged wine—wine that we will enjoy and that we will give to others.

QUESTIONS FOR REFLECTION AND DISCUSSION

1. How would you describe your current season of life? If you have retired, how has that experience been for you? If you are not retired, what changes do you anticipate retirement will bring? If you do not plan to retire, how will that be for you?

2. What image do you like best to describe where you are in the process of aging: leaves falling off a tree; a tree blossoming again; vintage wine; old or new wineskins? What does this image reveal to you about the aging process? What does this image reveal to you about your own responses to aging?

3. How do you respond to the descriptions of life as productive or fruitful? How do these descriptions contradict each other, and how do they complement each other? Which description is more accurate for your own life now?

A PERSONAL MEDITATION:
A DIFFERENT KIND OF RETIREMENT

Spend some time in God's presence with these questions. There are no right or wrong, good or bad, answers. Take whatever time you need to muse about your thoughts and feelings as you answer the questions that capture your attention.

1. Look out the window. If you can see a tree, spend some time noticing the way the tree reflects your experience as you age. If there is not a tree out your window, look for something else that reminds you of the aging process. Spend some time talking with God about how you feel about getting older.

2. Look at the apostle Paul's list of the fruits of the Spirit: love, joy, peace, patience, kindness, goodness, faithfulness, gentleness, and self-control (Galatians 5:22-23). Which fruits would you particularly like to be present in your life in your senior years?

- In what relationships would these fruits be most likely to show up? How would this be different for you from the way you lived in your younger years?
- Which parts of your life seem to be providing fruit-producing "sap" to you and others as you age?

3. How do you feel about the possibility that God may be saving the best wine for last in your life? Why might that sound like good news or bad news?

- What activities and relationships "pair" well with your life now? Who seems to be asking you for your wine? How do you feel about offering your new wine?

2

EXPERIENCING NEW BIRTH AS WE AGE

WHEN I WAS SIXTEEN, I asked Jesus into my heart. I expected to live happily ever after now that I was born again. Since then, I have learned it is more complicated than that. Being born again is an image Jesus used to describe what it means to enter into a new, everlasting relationship with God. But just as human babies change, grow up, and learn new things about themselves and about life, so we grow up spiritually. We change, living out our faith in unexpected ways. As I age, Jesus' description of being born again continues to be helpful to me. I am coming to believe that Jesus invites us to be "born again" in every season of life, perhaps especially in our senior years.

When Jesus spoke to Nicodemus about being born again, Nicodemus asked, "How can someone be born when they are old? Surely they cannot enter a second time into their mother's womb to be born!" (John 3:4). I am glad he asked that question because Jesus' reply speaks to me about my sense of continuing to be born again now that I am old. *How*, I might ask Jesus, *can this happen? How can I experience new life in old age?* Jesus might say to me what he said to Nicodemus—that new life, new birth, will be the work of the Holy Spirit.

"Flesh gives birth to flesh," Jesus said, "but the Spirit gives birth to spirit" (John 3:6). We are growing into who we are all our lives. We have already experienced new birth in other seasons of our lives. Now, as we age, our bodies are failing, but the Holy Spirit is still giving new life to our spirits. In our senior years, God invites us to look even more carefully for the work of the Holy Spirit in the inner being. Like Nicodemus, we can come to Jesus and ask him to tell us more. *Who is the Holy Spirit? And how can we recognize the work of the Spirit in our lives?*

Most of us know that the Holy Spirit is the "third person" in the Trinity. While this is a truth we say we believe, we may have reached our senior years with limited appreciation for how the Holy Spirit influences us and invites us to ongoing experiences of transformation. If what Jesus said is true (and I believe it is), then we will need to continue to look for the inner witness of the Spirit, to learn to listen for the whispers of the Holy Spirit to our spirits, and to recognize the presence of the Holy Spirit in our lives in this new season of aging, growth, and, yes, being born again.

Recognizing the Spirit's presence and hearing the Spirit's whispers means admitting that there is so much we cannot see, control, or predict. Jesus said to Nicodemus, "The wind blows wherever it pleases. You hear its sound, but you cannot tell where it comes from or where it is going. So it is with everyone born of the Spirit" (John 3:8). Teaching, once again with an image, Jesus said that the activity of the Spirit is like the blowing wind. In fact, the same Greek word means both wind and spirit. We can see the effects of the wind, but we don't know its beginning or its end. Our best weather forecasts do not always accurately predict the wind. We cannot control the Spirit of God any more than we can control the wind. There will always be some mystery in the work of the Spirit. But we can learn, by God's grace, to pay attention to the wind of the Spirit in our lives.

Another description of the work of the Holy Spirit appears much earlier in the Bible, in the second verse of Genesis. "Now the earth was formless and empty, darkness was over the surface of the deep, and the Spirit of God was hovering over the waters" (Genesis 1:2). I love the picture of the Spirit "hovering" over the earth before it was fully formed. From our vantage point at the beginning or middle of our senior years, the rest of life may look "formless and empty." It may even look dark and empty, and it is certainly unformed. But God the Holy Spirit is hovering over us, forming us, and giving us life and light, just as God the Holy Spirit formed the earth at the beginning of time. What a comfort that is.

NOTICING GOD'S PRESENCE AS WE CHANGE

We have the benefit of observing the work of the Holy Spirit in all the books of the Bible that come after Genesis—in the lives of the Israelites, in the inspiration of the Psalms, and in the instructions of the prophets. In the New Testament, we read about the Holy Spirit in the teaching of Jesus. Specifically, Jesus taught his disciples that the Spirit not only works in us but actually lives in us. The Holy Spirit, he said, "lives with you and will be in you" (John 14:17). Because the Spirit lives in us, Jesus was able to promise the disciples, "I will not leave you as orphans" (John 14:18). This is important to know as we age. Older people often feel the loneliness of orphans, as we retire and leave our professional colleagues, as friends move away, as our parents die and our children get busier and busier. But Jesus said he will not abandon us. The Holy Spirit will be with us and live in us. In our senior years, we may be surprised to find that the work of the Holy Spirit continues to change us.

Truth be told, some days I feel like I have so far to go before I really notice all that the Holy Spirit is offering me. On those days, God may remind me of some of the implications of my new birth as I age. As we age, change, and are born again, we look a lot like newborn babies. We find ourselves dependent on others, physically and emotionally. We may stumble as we try to walk into the unknown (or into the kitchen). Our family and friends can probably see the physical changes we are experiencing. They know that they need to speak up for us to hear well and that we need more light to read, but they may not be able to see the changes on the inside. They may not know that we keep growing and changing in our inner beings. We need people around us to love us and to help us process what these changes mean.

We need people who listen well to us as we experience new birth in our old age.

We are entering a new way of life, very different from the familiarity of our earlier life. Like a baby leaving the womb, we are leaving the only life we have known. Sometimes when I think of all that is changing in my life, the first thing out of my mouth is a cry. My cry reminds me that I am being born again. On those days, I can look at what Paul said in his letter to the Ephesians. God works in us, "not by pushing us around but by working within us, his Spirit deeply and gently within us" (Ephesians 3:21, MSG). I remember, then, that God understands the fragility of my new life and responds with love and gentleness.

I also remember one other similarity to newborn babies. Newborns, experts tell us, can hear quite well. The inner ear of newborn babies is fully developed. I hope this is true, spiritually, as I experience new birth in old age. My physical hearing may be declining, but I hope the inner ear of my soul can hear the persistent whispers of the Holy Spirit.

Speaking to his disciples, who were worried about him leaving them, Jesus called the Holy Spirit the Spirit of truth. "I have much more to say to you," he said.

"More than you can now bear. But when he, the Spirit of truth, comes, he will guide you into all the truth" (John 16:12-13). This is such good news. Not only will the Spirit repeat what we need to hear but the timing will be perfect. Jesus reminded the disciples that more truth would be too much for them to bear at the time. So he promised to send the Spirit of truth to guide them into truth when they were ready to hear it.

By now we have a lifetime of experiences behind us but we may not have heard all the Spirit wants to say. As we age and are born again yet another time, the Spirit continues to teach us truth. We may find we are more available and ready to listen. But we learn and listen in different ways. We may not be inclined to read as many theology books, or to listen to as many exciting testimonies, or to go to conferences about new ideas and perspectives. If we feel overwhelmed by all that we might be missing, we can be comforted by these words of Jesus. The Holy Spirit will continue to whisper what we are able to hear.

NEW WAYS TO LISTEN

When Jesus' disciples had been listening to him teach for some time, he asked them who they thought he really was. When pressed, Peter finally said, "You're the Christ, the Messiah, the Son of the living God" (Matthew 16:16, MSG).

Jesus' response to Peter startles me. He said, "Blessed are you, Simon son of Jonah, for this was not revealed to you by flesh and blood, but by my Father in heaven" (Matthew 16:17). Translated into our current vernacular, Jesus said, "God bless you, Simon, son of Jonah! You didn't get that answer out of books or from teachers. My Father in heaven, God himself, let you in on this secret of who I really am" (Matthew 16:17, MSG). This must have been an important moment because Jesus even changed Simon's name—to Peter—after he confirmed his declaration.

Jesus' words to Peter surprise me because I love books. I will be forever grateful for the hundreds of books I have read and for the many, many teachers who have taught me and enriched my faith. Is Jesus anti-books? Antiteaching? What was Jesus talking about?

As I am being born again in this season of life, I am noticing that God is inviting me to new ways of hearing truth, a reorientation on my faith journey. This invitation echoes what God said to Jeremiah after the Israelites returned from exile: "This is the covenant I will make with the house of Israel." God said, "I will put my law within them, and I will write it on their hearts. . . . No longer shall they teach one another, or say to each other, 'Know the LORD,' for they shall all know me" (Jeremiah 31:33-34, NRSV). Wow. I need to think about that.

When I was young and still living in "Egypt," God led me by the hand with detailed instructions about how I should live. For me, most of those instructions came from others, from books, and from teachers. I learned to look outside myself to hear the word of the Lord. I tried to listen to the inner witness of the Holy Spirit, but I was too young to have very many experiences of what that was like. And I didn't trust my ability to discern the Spirit's voice. Now God seems to be inviting me to listen more carefully to what the Holy Spirit is saying to me in my inner being. Perhaps as I age, I am expanding my experience of the four ways of wisdom suggested by John Wesley's famous Quadrilateral: We learn wisdom from Scripture, from church tradition, from the reasoning of our minds, and, ultimately, from the leading of the Spirit. All four ways of learning have shaped who I am, but as I age, I am being reminded again and again to listen to God's gentle whispers from the Holy Spirit.

I hold this new way of listening carefully in my soul. Sometimes I ask myself, *What if I think I am listening to the Spirit, and I make a mistake?* I always compare what I think I am hearing to what I have learned throughout my life. I remember that Jesus taught his disciples that his sheep know his voice (John 10:1-6). I try to hear that voice amid the many other voices in my life. Usually this means that I need to sit still and wait until one thought or feeling separates itself and seems to silently echo Jesus' voice in my mind and heart. I compare that echo with the words of Scripture to see if it might be Jesus' voice speaking to me through the Holy Spirit. Sometimes I talk this over with close friends or a spiritual director. Then, in all honesty, I "experiment" with the truths I am hearing to see if they bear the fruits of the Spirit in my life. After all, Jesus said that "by their fruit" we will know who is telling the truth (Matthew 7:15-20). When I see "good fruit" in my life, I rejoice that I have recognized the voice of Jesus.

This way of listening is very personal, and I am finding it is very much part of my own aging experience. As I sit in stillness and quiet, the Spirit may remind me of a verse I memorized in another season of my life. Sometimes the Spirit brings back to my attention a truth from a book I read or a talk I heard years ago, and I hear that truth now in a new, more personal way. Sometimes the Spirit simply reminds me that God loves me, even though I feel weak or inadequate. Other times the Spirit whispers "peace" to my soul in a way that "passes all understanding" (Philippians 4:7, RSV). Changing my orientation inward rather than always looking outward feels like being born again. And it feels like I am learning to walk all over again. But rather than stumbling away from God, listening to the Spirit in this way is leading me to a much deeper experience of God's love. I will need to spend the rest of my life listening.

THE LONG ROAD TO TODAY

Of course, I did not know any of this that day I sat in my bedroom being born again for the first time. I never, ever could have imagined the journey I was embarking on. I remember the day when I read in King James English the words the apostle Paul recorded in the book of Galatians: "I am crucified with Christ: nevertheless I live; yet not I, but Christ liveth in me" (Galatians 2:20, KJV). First of all, I was excited that I actually found the book of Galatians. Then I thought, *Wow. This is good. If I ask Jesus into my heart, the "old" me will be dead, crucified with Christ. Now I can become a new person.* I thought this would happen immediately. I would be a "good Christian," impressing the world with my spirituality and my love.

It didn't happen like that. In fact, my efforts to be a good Christian were such a failure that I entered my first experience of depression. I didn't know it was the cry of my baby soul in the labor and delivery room, but I knew I was miserable. I was born again, but the reality of my day-to-day life was that I didn't understand what was happening, and I believed I would never be good enough to please God. There were many causes behind my depression: the high standards of my parents, my temperamental propensity to self-doubt, my misunderstanding of what faith in Christ meant, and, especially, my fear of disappointing God. I lived with depression crouching at my door for at least twenty years. Even as I tried to grow in my faith, I kept bumping into doubt and self-judgment. In the following years, God healed my depression, thanks to the mysterious wind of the Holy Spirit, thanks to the love of God given to me through my family and friends, and thanks to a gifted counselor. I have also learned new, rather simple words for what I didn't understand as a young person.

THE FALSE SELF AND THE TRUE SELF

As an adult, I learned about the false self and the true self. I learned that everyone struggles with the tension between these two selves. The false self is the person we wish we were, the person we think we should be but aren't. The false self is the person who wants to impress others with the gifts God has given us. We rarely know it, but the false self is ego driven and self-serving. The false self is defensive, protecting the image we want to project. The false self is full of pride. The reason we don't recognize our false self is because, through our good works and holy behavior, the false self masquerades as an angel of light (2 Corinthians 11:14-15).

The true self, on the other hand, is the person God created us to be, full of God's gifts, full of the talents God has given us, and full of God's grace and love. Paul wrote that in Christ, we have "taken off [the] old self . . . and have put on the new self" (Colossians 3:9-10). This new self, John wrote, is "born not of natural descent, nor of human decision . . . but born of God" (John 1:13). Because the true self is created by God, it lives freely. It does not need to control things in order to protect a self-image. The fruits of the Holy Spirit seem to flow out of who we are, often surprising us.

The tension between the true self and false self has been with us throughout our lives, from young adulthood, through midlife, and into our senior years. And as we age, the false self grows old with us. I wonder if another purpose of the aging journey is to give us more time to recognize the egotistical lure of the false self in ways we could not see in our younger years. And as we age, we also have the opportunity to see the fruits of the true self, which were hidden in our younger years by the glitter of the false self. This will take a lifetime because the false self tells us lies and teaches us to lie. Jesus did not use the terms *false self* and *true self*, but he did talk about the lies of the Great Deceiver. He said to his followers, "If you hold to my teaching, you are really my disciples. Then you will know the truth, and the truth will set you free" (John 8:31-32). Those listening challenged him that they had never been slaves and did not need to be set free. He said (for our ears and for theirs), "Why is my language not clear to you? Because you are unable to hear what I say. You belong to your father, the devil. . . . There is no truth in him. When he lies, he speaks his native language, for he is a liar and the father of lies" (John 8:43-44).

Strong words from the Son of God. They remind me

that my own native language, the language of my false self, is full of lies I have believed for decades. And Jesus' words remind me that I usually do not know that I am enslaved by these lies. But the truth will set me free if I can admit to the lies of my false self. Here is a short list of the lies I have lived with and bring into this season of life:

I must be always right, correct, biblical, and proper.

I can and must meet every need of those I love.

God is waiting for me to shape up, use the right words in prayer, and grow into holiness before he will listen to me.

I should always be frugal and efficient.

If I am a good Christian, I will help in my church whenever needed.

I should never, ever be angry, misinformed, tired, or weak.

And I should never, ever disappoint God or those I love and respect.

The list could go on and on. Lies like this are so familiar to me, I usually don't even know when I am believing them. Psychologist David Benner writes that "the false self is like the air we breathe. We have become so accustomed to its presence that we are no longer aware of it."[1]

The concept of the true self and the false self helps me understand the conundrum I felt early in my Christian life. When I was born again as a teenager, my false self was fighting me all the way. I didn't know the terms *false self* and *true self*, but I knew that, as Paul wrote to the Romans, I had "the desire to do what is good," but I could not carry it out; I could not do "the good I want[ed] to do" (Romans 7:18-19). My false self and my true self were at war with each other.

Recently I read again the verses from Galatians that I discovered all those years ago. This time I read the passage in a different translation. This new translation describes much of my experience of being born again in my senior years. Paul wrote:

> I tried keeping rules and working my head off to please God, and it didn't work. . . . I have been crucified with Christ. My ego is no longer central. It is no longer important that I appear righteous before you or have your good

opinion, and I am no longer driven to impress God. Christ lives in me.

GALATIANS 2:19-20, MSG

I could not have embraced these truths, translated in this way, in my teenage years. I believed I had been crucified with Christ and that Christ lived in me. But I barely knew my ego. I didn't know about the lies my false self believed. I didn't know that I was desperate to appear righteous, please my peers, and impress others. But the physical diminishments of age have taught me much. For all of us, the aging process invites us to let go of false ways of looking at ourselves, at others, and even at our own faith practices.

In these precious years of growing older, the Holy Spirit wants to teach us that we do not need to keep our old and familiar self-made rules, we do not need to impress people, and we do not need to bow down to our ego. The Spirit whispers truth to us: The false self is crucified with Christ, Christ lives in us, and Christ loves others through us. This is the Good News. As we experience the loss of the values of our false self, we discover a new self, a self that has been born again.

QUESTIONS FOR REFLECTION AND DISCUSSION

1. When did you first hear the term "being born again"? How does this term clarify the experiences of spiritual growth in your own life? Or is there another way to describe your journey with more clarity?

2. How would you describe your experience of the "indwelling" of the Holy Spirit? In what ways is this something new for you, and in what ways has it been part of your experience for years?

   What strikes you about Jesus' words to the disciples, "I have much more to say to you, more than you can now bear. But when he, the Spirit of truth, comes, he will guide you into all the truth" (John 16:12-13)? Can you think of a time when the Holy Spirit repeated truth to you that you couldn't hear the first time?

3. How do you think the false self grows old with us as we age? What things have you found that help you nourish your true self?

A PERSONAL MEDITATION:
EXPERIENCING NEW BIRTH AS WE AGE

As you muse on questions that intrigue you, remember to take your time. Listen for the whispers of the Holy Spirit to your spirit within.

1. "Now the earth was formless and empty, darkness was over the surface of the deep, and the Spirit of God was hovering over the waters" (Genesis 1:2). Picture in your mind the creation of the earth. How does your own experience of aging seem formless or dark?

   • Think of two or three ways the Holy Spirit hovers over your life. What feelings do you have about the Holy Spirit's work in your life today?

2. How have the true self and the false self influenced your own spiritual journey?

   • What words describe your own false self and true self?

- How are you experiencing both perspectives in your senior years?

3. How do you respond to Paul's words in Galatians 2:19-20 (MSG)?

> What actually took place is this: I tried keeping rules and working my head off to please God, and it didn't work. . . . Indeed, I have been crucified with Christ. My ego is no longer central. It is no longer important that I appear righteous before you or have your good opinion, and I am no longer driven to impress God. Christ lives in me.

- What catches your attention in these words that could be an invitation from God to you?
- How might the invitation apply to something you are experiencing this week?

3

HOLY LOSSES, HOLY INVITATIONS

EVEN IF WE KNOW theoretically that there are benefits coming with aging, the reality is that most of us will probably resist getting older. The first signs of aging happening usually appear in the mirror. (*Where did that gray hair come from? When did gravity start working on my body?*) Then we start to notice that we have less energy for things that used to seem so easy. (*How do those young people keep up with their kids?*) Sometimes we are reminded of our age by those who no longer want our help. ("That's okay. We have a new person in the office to do that job.") In short, getting older does not have a good reputation.

Most of us associate age with loss. The loss of hearing, eyesight, and muscle tone. The loss of a fulfilling job, the daily run, and personal independence. And the loss of long-term relationships. Some of us are aware of these losses early in the process, on the brink of our senior years. Other people only fear them from a distance. Whenever these experiences begin, at some point most of us ask, *Why in the world would anyone want to grow old?* We wonder how it is that someone can say, "For the benefit of who we are and what we may become, it's good to experience old age." Or even more astounding, we might ask how it is possible to say of an older person, "she moved consciously into elderhood as an anticipated stage of growth, rather than as a punishment for having outlived her usefulness."[1] How can this be? How is it that this season of life could be part of God's plan? Why does God allow us to lose so much as we age? Why is death a part of life? And, even more confounding, how can we celebrate this season of life?

When I began my foray into exploring the aging process, I started asking my friends how they were preparing to grow old. Some said they were all set—they had set up their wills and had a good financial planner. Others told me they weren't worried. After retirement, they had found part-time jobs and were making plans to travel. They have enough energy and enough opportunities to re-create their activities and priorities. In fact, for some, retirement becomes a land of opportunity. We all experience retirement and aging in our own way. I celebrate with these friends.

But for others, the losses of our senior years run deep. Illness, lifestyle changes, and disappointed expectations weigh heavily. Some people have experienced significant loss by midlife. (These people often seem wise beyond their years.) For others, the losses aren't obvious until their sixties and don't press upon them until their seventies or even eighties. But the reality is that for all of us who are getting older, even those who enjoy retirement, there will be changes in our lives that we do not like. All of us need to navigate around the reality of aging, denial of what we don't like, and acceptance of where we are in the process. As I began to experience some of these changes, I found myself wanting to dialogue with others about what they were expecting, what they feared, and what they were already experiencing. Bruce was someone who understood what I was asking.

Still in his fifties, Bruce said that he was trying to prepare for the losses of aging. As dismal as that sounded,

I was intrigued. What did he mean by that? His reply: "I want to notice the losses already happening in my life so I can learn from them. I don't want the losses to define me. If I practice holding things loosely as I go along, perhaps the losses that come with age won't be so devastating. At least I'll be more used to them."

I could relate to that. When I saw old age coming down the pike, I began to think about the losses and changes I had already experienced. Intuitively I knew that past experiences of loss would teach me as I aged. God had used losses in transformative ways in my life. Letting go of what I thought I needed allowed me to receive what God wanted to give. I am thankful for that. But underneath my youthful losses, there are losses in aging that are much more difficult to receive. As I age, I want to embrace these internal, underneath losses because perhaps they, too, by God's grace, are part of God's design for me and part of the benefits of old age in my life.

LET ME COUNT THE LOSSES

Things I used to do quickly, I do slowly. It is much harder to multitask. My eyesight is not as sharp. My brain has less space for details. I make more and simpler to-do lists. I am retired from cooking. (I can still "fix" a dinner when necessary, but thankfully it isn't necessary very often.) I no longer drive seventy-five miles an hour on the interstate. I have fewer hours in my days because I need more hours in my nights—to say nothing of the hours spent in medical appointments. But the losses are not just counted in abilities or hours and minutes. I am also losing my sense of who I am, of what validates me. My sense, so far, is that it is not so much that my core identity is changing as it is that my view of myself is changing.

In my adult life, I worked in campus ministry and later served as a conference speaker, a premarital counselor, a workshop presenter, a church leader, and a spiritual director. I was smart, busy, and really quite capable. At least, I used to think I was. Many activities have fallen by the wayside, and new, less familiar ones are taking their place. I am still a spiritual director, but those times are carefully scheduled between grandparental duties, activities with my now-retired husband, and—dare I say?—naps.

There is also the loss of my ability to be available to others. I used to stay up late at night to help out when I was needed. Now the needs I offer to meet have to come before dinner. I used to have many talents to help me respond creatively to a variety of requests. Now some of those talents are a bit worn-out and some of them no longer bring me joy. I used to congratulate myself at how helpful, available, and capable I was. Now the self-congratulations sound hollow.

I ask myself almost daily, *Am I really okay with this? Why is God allowing the losses to multiply? How can I accept these losses with grace and contentment?* Accepting old age is a moving target because every day I get older. Every day I need to look at my life with fresh eyes. I need to understand and accept as much of the aging process as I can. I am finding that I usually need to start with accepting my aging body.

LISTENING TO THE SILENT MESSAGES OF OUR BODIES

Even those who see retirement through a very positive and optimistic lens notice, about the time of retirement, that their bodies start to change. We probably notice our bodies first because our bodies don't lie, and changes in our bodies are usually out of our control.

After our recent move to Colorado, I was pleased to find a gym nearby where I could actually work the machines. Yesterday I pedaled away on the stationary bike while I watched a young woman on the treadmill in front of me. She had to have been fifty years younger than me, but that didn't stop me from thinking, *Who does she think she is, looking so great? What is wrong with me that I don't look like that?* I guess I have a way to go in embracing my older body! Years ago, someone reminded me that "the body accepts what the mind rejects." This was true for me when I first heard it, and it is certainly true as I face my senior years. My body is telling me things my brain does not want to hear.

I learned recently that this is because of my vagus nerve. (Who knew?!) David Brooks wrote in the *New York Times* about "The Wisdom Your Body Knows: You Are Not Just Thinking with Your Brain." According to the article, the vagus nerve "emerges from the brain stem and wanders across the heart, lungs, kidney and gut. The vagus nerve is one of the pathways through which the body and brain talk to each other in an unconscious conversation."[2] *In other words*, I said to myself, *perhaps my body, my gut, is speaking to me*. I have since learned that the "brain-gut connection" is getting a lot of press these days. Harvard Health Publishing reported that "the gut-brain connection is no joke."[3] Those of us who try to ignore our aging bodies and *think* our way out of old age are going down a misguided path.

David Brooks's column in the newspaper and my unkind thoughts in the gym remind me to listen to my body. I am learning things I can do to take care of my body and, specifically, my vagus nerve. Bill Simpson, in a newspaper column called "Aging for Amateurs," writes about "Taking Care of Our Vagus Nerves." Simpson credits our vagus nerves with helping to maintain healthy blood pressure, blood glucose, and cholesterol as well as lowering our risk for heart disease, stroke, and diabetes—to say nothing of our levels of anxiety and inflammation.[4]

The problem, according to my own amateur observations, is that we cannot feel our blood pressure, glucose level, or our cholesterol. And our kidneys, hearts, and lungs don't speak a familiar language. My brain is still talking like a fifty-year-old: *You can do it! Keep trying! Push harder!* My body responds (thanks to the vagus nerve): *Whoa! Slow down! Take care of yourself!* Listening to the silent experiences of my body is something I need to learn how to do. When I am tired, for instance, I need to learn to say to myself, *My body is telling me to slow down now—at least for a few minutes.* Perhaps my vagus nerve is reminding me that I cannot do every-thing I think needs to be done, or even what I think I want to do. Perhaps God, who created my body (with a vagus nerve), is speaking to me.

LISTENING WITH MY BODY FOR MY SOUL

I have learned that my newly discovered vagus nerve needs a lot of the same things my soul needs. Scientists tell us that we can improve our "vagal tone" by deep breathing, singing, and meditation, among other things. This reminds me of breath prayer, of hymns, and of meditation in Scripture and in prayer. Perhaps the same disciplines that keep my body strong are also good for my soul.

Just sitting and breathing deeply quiets our souls and our bodies. The idea of "breath prayer" is rooted in scriptural teaching. Genesis 2:7 tells us that God formed us from dust and then "breathed" into our nostrils the "breath of life," and we became living beings. After his resurrection, Jesus "breathed" on the disciples and said, "Receive the Holy Spirit" (John 20:21-23). Christians ever since have been taught the value of "breath prayer." As we sit in peace and silence, we are invited to breathe deeply. As we breathe, we may remember that God created us and that Jesus breathes the Spirit into our lives, even today. We may want to breathe in and out as we remember a verse from the Bible. Or we may not want to think at all. We just breathe. Deep breathing is good for our souls and apparently good for our vagus nerves.

We may also attend to both our vagus nerves and our souls with music. Experts tell us that our bodies and our brains are attuned to the notes of the musical scales. Music, they say, can have a medicinal effect on our bodies. Kirstin Butler's article "This Is Your Body on Music" describes at length the effect of music on our bodies. She notes that today there is "an enormous and growing body of research [that] attempts to talk specifically about just how and why music affects us so much."[5]

As with most experiences of our bodies and souls, the effect of music is uniquely personal. My husband is enriched by a variety of classical music. It is more life-giving to me to listen to Christian songs, especially those with the words of Scripture. I suspect my grandchildren are drawn to very, very different music. But whatever kind of music we love, it is no surprise that God invites us to experience music for the health of our bodies and our souls. The Bible tells us to "sing and make music from your heart to the Lord" (Ephesians 5:19). Those of us (like me) who are not very musical can give health to our bodies and enrich our souls even when we just listen to music. Others have the skills to play music, sing music, and participate in musical performances with groups. Whatever our ability, God invites us to be drawn by the Holy Spirit through music into a deeper relationship with God.

Or we may choose to nourish our bodies and souls by meditating. For Christians, the idea of meditation can be both welcoming and intimidating. We may think of "meditation" as emptying our minds, sitting for long periods of time, and shutting out all thoughts that seem to interfere with the purity of our expectations. It helps to demystify the term. Using the term broadly, we are meditating as we sit and breathe deeply. We are meditating as we listen to music. And, especially, we are meditating as we engage with Scripture and prayer. Most of us, as we age, discover that we have had experiences of meditation throughout our years of discipleship and spiritual formation. We may not have called it meditation, and we probably didn't realize that it was good for our bodies as well as our souls. Now, in our senior years, we can be thankful that meditation was strengthening our vagus nerves before we even knew it.

Learning to experience meditation that includes Scripture and prayer is a gift at any age, but one that we may have more time to engage in as we age. One meaningful way to include meditative Bible reading in our lives is with the practice of Lectio Divina. This way of reading Scripture works especially well for me because it is simple and specific, and it makes it easier for me to remember the whispers of the Spirit as I go throughout my day. Lectio Divina means "Divine Reading" in Latin, and most descriptions of this practice are translated from Latin. As I have lived with this form of meditating over the years, I have come up with my own description of Lectio Divina, in English. This works well for me:

Read a short passage of Scripture.
Notice a word or phrase that stands out to you.
Meditate on how that word or phrase might apply
    to some part of your life today.
Notice the invitation of God to you in that passage
    of Scripture.

Reading this way is, first of all, slow. We may be reading very familiar Scripture, but we dare not skim over it. When we take time to allow our minds to wander through the passage, to notice what word or phrase captures our attention, and then sit quietly musing about what God might be saying to us through this word or phrase, then we are meditating. What we experience is often beyond what we can describe in words. The title of author Thelma Hall's book on Lectio Divina is *Too Deep for Words*. That is so true. Experiencing Scripture in this way is often too deep for words.

Lectio Divina often leads to prayer, another form of meditation. Praying meditatively is different from the more familiar way of praying where we (unfortunately) give God a "to-do" list of ways we would like him to solve our problems. Or perhaps we make a lot of suggestions about how God could solve the world's problems. Meditative prayer is more reflective of our personal communion with our Father. We may try to express what we are experiencing in that moment. We might say, if we are using words, "Today I am thankful for . . ." Or we might say, "Today, I am anxious about . . ."—or whatever thought or emotion comes to mind that we would like to share with God. It is as though the Holy Spirit is saying to us, "How are you today?" We may choose to respond in silence, knowing that "[our] Father knows what [we] need before [we] ask him" (Matthew 6:8). Prayer like this may start out with words and end in wordless mystery. It is waiting quietly in God's presence.

After I read and pray, I might continue the meditative experience by returning to deep breathing or music. When I meditate in this way, I am transformed by God's love. I have much more to learn, but I am thankful that all of this is good for my body and also so good for my soul.

A FIRST EXPERIENCE OF LECTIO

If you are unfamiliar with this way of reading Scripture, try reading Isaiah 42:16 in this way.

> I will lead the blind by ways they have not known,
>   along unfamiliar paths I will guide them;
> I will turn the darkness into light before them
>   and make the rough places smooth.
> These are the things I will do;
>   I will not forsake them.

1. Start by being quiet, taking several very deep breaths.

2. Read the verse slowly two times, perhaps once out loud.
3. Which word or phrase stands out to you?
4. How might this word or phrase speak into some situation or relationship in your life today?
5. How might God be inviting you to transformation in this verse?
6. Be quiet. Breathe deeply. Receive God's invitation.

OUR AGING GIFTEDNESS

The aging process is multilayered and involves listening to how age affects our spiritual gifts, our temperamental preferences, and our professional skill sets. By the time we are in our sixties and seventies, most of us have taken multiple personality tests that promise to tell us who we are. But as we age, we change. We have been changing all our lives, but many of us find that the changes of age surprise us and seem to accumulate year by year. As our lives slow down with retirement and physical changes, we find ourselves asking questions we have never asked before. What is an extrovert to do when he finds he wants to stay home instead of go out to be with people? What is a loyal church member to do when her gifts can no longer be used in the church kitchen, in the church pulpit, or on the church board? What happens when the corporate executive no longer enjoys business meetings? What happens to our gifts and preferences now? We have so much to learn as we age.

One of the inventories many of us took in our younger years is called "StrengthsFinder" (now known as "CliftonStrengths"). This inventory is immensely helpful to people looking to discover their giftedness. We learn from StrengthsFinder what our God-given strengths are. The inventory gives insights that are rich and life-giving. But as we age, we may well find ourselves asking difficult questions about our experience of these strengths. What happens when the strengths we have to offer are no longer requested? What happens when our deepest preferences and gifts no longer give us joy and satisfaction? Or, perhaps even harder, what happens when we notice that our strengths are waning? Does this mean we are losing our very identity as we age? I hope not!

We can be comforted by the apostle Paul's words to the church at Corinth as he struggled with a weakness that God would not remove. Paul's conclusion is surprising. "When I am weak," he said, "then I am strong" (2 Corinthians 12:10). Paul may not have been "old" by our standards, and we probably experienced weaknesses in our own younger years, but as we age, unremitting emotional and physical weaknesses often become a daily struggle. Is it really true, as this same verse says in *The Message*, that "the weaker I get, the stronger I become"? The answer, I believe, is definitely "Yes!"—but it is ever so difficult to come by.

It is difficult because one of the things we all do, young and old alike, is to become enamored with our own gifts. We generally like our gifts, probably more than we admit. They have helped us do things well. But as we age and begin experiencing fewer opportunities and less energy to use our gifts, we may respond in unhealthy ways. If we are gifted, for instance, with gifts in leadership, we may grasp at leadership opportunities and complain that others aren't doing things the right way. If we are gifted in wisdom, we may feel that our perspective is the gold standard for what is accurate and bemoan that people aren't asking for our opinion as much as they used to. For people who are especially gifted in helping others, it may seem impossible to not jump in and fix things, even if we get in the way. In short, we risk becoming addicted to our gifts and to the way we have always used them. It is not that we will no longer use these gifts as we age but that we will probably use them in new ways, and we will need to learn to hold them more loosely. We will need divine help to be transformed as we experience losses in our bodies and our giftedness.

I asked my friend Ann how she is handling losses like these. Ann is an extrovert and has always had lots of energy. She did more in one career than I could do in a lifetime. I asked her what it was like for her to lose some of that energy. Specifically, I asked her about what she experienced as she aged from a young fifty to the ripe old age of seventy. She said she started out the aging process with a strong body. When she had health issues, she assumed her body would always get better. She just needed to wait it out. That worked until she was about sixty. Then she had surgery. Recovery seemed to take forever. Then another surgery. Then more health issues. More surgery and longer and longer recoveries. Her losses seemed insurmountable.

Using her dynamic and familiar gifts wasn't working anymore. I asked her what had been helpful to her in the losses that came with the diminishment of her physical energy. Her response reminded me again of how our aging bodies influence the way we experience our giftedness. Ann said, "I found out it is not helpful when I don't stop long enough to engage with what my body is trying to tell me." Trained as a nurse, she knew that she should listen to her body, but she never had to do that in her younger years. "Now my body says rest, but my mind says I should still be productive. Sometimes I feel as though I've lost all my capacity to get things done." For Ann, not being productive is one of the hardest parts of having an aging body.

I get that. As our bodies slow us down, we "should" ourselves. We tell ourselves we should do so much more than we are able to do. We should be just like our younger selves, even as we watch ourselves age. Ann said she expected to live her life as she always had. Eventually this led her into depression—an experience she had not had before. Her story reminds me of Proverbs 13:12, "Hope deferred makes the heart sick." As we age, we are likely to be disappointed again and again by our reduced energy and our changing abilities. These disappointed expectations make us sick. For Ann, this took the form of depression.

Ann and I have had many cups of coffee talking about how we can respond to all of this. One thing we have noticed is that we both have more clarity about what doesn't work than about what does work. Here is my own list of what doesn't work:

- It doesn't work to deny the changes in our bodies and in our lives. They are going to happen anyway.
- It doesn't work to resist the changes and losses. Resistance takes up a lot of energy, which we have in lesser and lesser amounts.
- It doesn't work to drop out, complain, or push harder. These are passive, or passive-aggressive, ways to respond to aging.
- It doesn't work to lunge, grasp, or artificially create opportunities primarily for our own satisfaction.

GRIEVING THE LOSSES

One of the things that *does* work in accepting our losses is grieving them. My list of things that don't work tells me things about my life that I wish weren't true. I do not like that I am no longer the strong person I used to be. My list speaks of my own places of denial about my age. But if I am going to make headway out of this self-deception, I need to admit the truth and learn how to grieve my losses.

Grieving is another part of life with a bad reputation. Who wants to be unhappy? Our friends often try to talk us out of our sadness. ("You don't look that old. I think you are doing great. You should be counting your blessings!") We try to distract ourselves with entertainment, the internet, even trying to be helpful when we are not needed. But all that we do to avoid our grief is a dead-end street. Grief unembraced is not transformational. It is also not biblical.

The Bible encourages us to look honestly at our grief and our losses. Ecclesiastes 7:2 reminds us, "It is better to go to a house of mourning than to go to a house of feasting." Grief is a stark reality of human lives. God called David "a man after [his] own heart" (Acts 13:22). But this man, gifted by God in so many ways, was able to pour out his grief: "Listen to my prayer, O God. . . . My thoughts trouble me and I am distraught. . . . My heart is in anguish within me. . . . Fear and trembling have beset me; horror has overwhelmed me" (Psalm 55:1-5). Jesus was "a man of sorrows, and acquainted with grief" (Isaiah 53:3, KJV). Paul experienced the grief of unhealed pain. When he prayed about this, God's reply was not to heal Paul but to promise him, "My grace is sufficient for you, for my power is made perfect in weakness" (2 Corinthians 12:9). God did not seem to answer Paul's prayers. At least, not in the way he hoped. The deep, mysterious grace of God in our own losses is that as we grieve, we will be invited to accept what we cannot change and experience God's promise that his strength "comes into its own" in our weakness (2 Corinthians 12:9, MSG). In our grief, we allow ourselves to be sad about all that we cannot keep as we age. This is an ongoing process, but Scripture reminds us that God wants to hear our cries and concerns.

Most of us have heard of the five stages of grief, identified by psychiatrist Elisabeth Kübler-Ross: denial, anger, bargaining, depression, and acceptance. Knowing about these stages is immensely helpful to people who have lost a loved one to death. They can also be helpful to us as we navigate the losses that often come with age. We can notice what things we are doing to try to deny our age. We can notice when we are angry about what we cannot do. We can notice when we bargain with ourselves and others to try to circumvent our losses. Like Ann, some of us may go through a time of depression when we despair that life as we knew it is over.

Grief counselors remind us that these "stages" of

grief are not linear. We weave in and out of these phases of grieving, whether the losses come because of death or (I would say) as we age. There are days when we experience the grief of our losses in new and fresh ways. But there will also be days when, by God's grace, we move toward acceptance of what is happening to us and begin to find peace.

HOLY INVITATIONS

I am slowly learning that buried in our losses are holy invitations. These invitations are personal and come addressed to us each individually. Even as I struggle with the losses of aging, I want to spend the rest of my life noticing and receiving whatever God is giving to me through the losses.

The apostle Paul gives us some hints about this. "We do not lose heart," he says. "Though outwardly we are wasting away . . . inwardly we are being renewed day by day" (2 Corinthians 4:16). One of the purposes of old age is to be renewed *inwardly*. "Even though on the outside it often looks like things are falling apart on us, on the inside, where God is making new life, not a day goes by without his unfolding grace" (2 Corinthians 4:16, MSG). As we age, we learn to offer ourselves to God for inward renewal. As we age, God invites us to notice new life on the inside as his grace unfolds in us every day. Paul wrote to the church at Rome: "I urge you . . . to offer your bodies as a living sacrifice, holy and pleasing to God—this is your true and proper worship" (Romans 12:1). As we get older, we are invited again and again to offer to God the diminishing parts of our bodies and to welcome the grace of inward renewal.

This perspective is counterintuitive culturally and spiritually. I recently climbed two flights of stairs in an old building to get to an office on the top floor. I was winded by the time I arrived for my appointment. By way of an excuse, I said to the receptionist, "Whew. That was a long way up. But I've never been old before." Not missing a beat, she reminded me: "Sometimes we just need to ignore our bodies and keep climbing."

What she said is common advice and affects us all. For those of us who are Christians, listening to ourselves as we age may be a spiritual stretch. We may believe it is not spiritual to acknowledge or, shall we say, succumb to the problems of age. We may fear that when we listen to our bodies, we are putting the temporary before the eternal. Or we struggle with a sense of guilt that we are being selfish or, worse yet, lazy. We are afraid we might be compromising important spiritual convictions. But quite the opposite is true.

At the heart of our Christian theology is the belief that *God became flesh*. John tells us that "the Word [God] became flesh and lived among us . . . full of grace and truth" (John 1:14, NRSV). In other words, God enfleshed grace and truth in a *human body*. Jesus lived in a body, just as we do. Then he died. His resurrection three days later is certainly the most wonderful promise of ultimate transformation. Many of our own losses as we age are mini-reminders of death. And many of the invitations hidden in our losses remind us of resurrection.

We also learn from Christian teaching that "[our] bodies are temples of the Holy Spirit" (1 Corinthians 6:19). The fact that the Spirit of God lives in our bodies, and yet our bodies are allowed to die, must give us pause. How can this be? This is counterintuitive indeed. But Paul reminds us: "Honor God with your bodies" (1 Corinthians 6:20). If I am going to age as a Jesus follower, I will need to learn to honor God with my aging body, even as I listen for the truths and invitations that come with the diminishments of age.

AN INVITATION IN THE NIGHT

One of my own experiences of hearing such an invitation happened in my early sixties. We all hear a variety of different invitations from God throughout our lives, but as I age, the invitations and losses seem to be coming more frequently. I heard one of my first during the night. Sleep has always been difficult for me, but about the time I turned sixty, insomnia came banging at my door. I lay awake every night for hours. Sometimes in anxiety, sometimes in boredom. I prayed every night that God would help me sleep. That didn't work. It only made my insomnia worse because then I would lie awake trying to solve the theological issues around unanswered prayer.

One tired morning as I sat in quiet, I began to wonder why God created us to sleep in the first place. If I were God, I would want people to stay awake to help take care of the world. But for about eight hours out of every twenty-four, God designed us to be asleep, unable to serve him and unable to get done all the things we would do if we were awake. While we are asleep, we are useless, and we are out of control. That thought caught my attention. In my fatigue, it occurred to me that even important people like CEOs and international heads of state need to sleep. Why would God do that? They all have more important things to do than to lie in bed for hours every night.

In the stillness of that morning, I realized that when I sleep, I am out of control. When I experience insomnia, I am also out of control. I certainly cannot make myself go to sleep. Perhaps insomnia and sleep accomplish the same purpose. In other words, insomnia was a reminder, like sleep, that we do not control our own lives, let alone the world. God is our Creator and is the one in charge. My "theology of sleep" is my own personal reminder that God is God and I am not. God is in control of my life, my waking and sleeping hours, in loving, creative, grace-filled ways. Apparently my being out of control is part of God's design.

I keep forgetting this. I need to come back to my reflections on insomnia again and again. I need to remind myself again and again what God taught me in the night: *I am not in charge of my life or the world; God is.* To my surprise, I have even come to treasure the experience of insomnia. I do some of my best thinking at night. I treasure the depth of love that I find in my insomniac hours. "Even at night my heart instructs me" (Psalm 16:7).

Not everyone struggles with insomnia in old age. We all have our own personal issues and problems, but with these losses come invitations to a deeper experience of God's love. For me, the loss of sleep included an invitation to something better.

HIDDEN TREASURES

When Bob and I visited Charleston, South Carolina, several years ago, we did what tourists do. We took a carriage ride through the historic district. The driver of the carriage was a young man (of course!) who was very proud of his city and the stories he could tell us. One of his stories was about Hurricane Hugo, the storm that devastated Charleston in 1989. When they were cleaning up the rubble from a historic church that had been destroyed, some of the workers found the cross that had been on the altar. As they lifted it from the ground, it was too heavy for one man to lift. Curious, they somehow looked inside the cross. There they found piles of gold, probably hidden from the enemy during the Civil War.

It doesn't take a lot of imagination to notice that the losses of old age are hidden in the Cross of Jesus. Our losses often feel like small deaths. But often, by God's grace to us, we notice that after the loss, after the death, there is resurrection. This resurrection comes in the form of new life that we did not know about in our younger years. Growing old becomes "the evidence of things not seen" (Hebrews 11:1, KJV) until we get there. The aging process gives us the opportunity to learn what it means to lose ourselves, to die to ourselves, and to experience new life.

QUESTIONS FOR REFLECTION AND DISCUSSION

1. What activities that used to be life-giving no longer energize you or bring you joy? How do changes like this affect you?

2. What connections have you noticed between your experiences with your body and your spiritual journey? What do you do that nourishes both your body and your soul?

3. What have you noticed about the loss of opportunities to use your gifts? How do you feel about that? What part of that experience is hardest for you, and what part has worked out well?

4. How do you respond to God's response to Paul, "My grace is sufficient for you, for my power is made perfect

in weakness" (2 Corinthians 12:9)? When are you most likely to experience strength in weakness? When are you least likely to experience this?

A PERSONAL MEDITATION:
HOLY LOSSES, HOLY INVITATIONS

Losing something in order to receive something is a difficult concept for most of us. But it is what Jesus suggested in the Beatitudes, which he taught to his disciples in the Sermon on the Mount. Spend time slowly responding to three of these Beatitudes.

1. Jesus said, "Blessed are the poor in spirit, for theirs is the kingdom of heaven" (Matthew 5:3). Or, according to pastor and scholar Eugene Peterson in *The Message*: "You're blessed when you're at the end of your rope. With less of you there is more of God and his rule." Think of an area in your life where you are "at the end of your rope." In what current circumstances or relationships do you feel stuck, unable to think or work your way out of the pain you feel?

- What invitation from God do you hear in the promise that "with less of you there is more of God"?

2. Jesus said, "Blessed are those who mourn, for they will be comforted" (Matthew 5:4). What things are you mourning as you grow older? In what ways have you "lost what is most dear to you" (Matthew 5:4, MSG)? How would you like to receive God's comfort as you mourn?

3. Jesus said, "Blessed are the meek, for they will inherit the earth" (Matthew 5:5). Or, according to *The Message*: "You're blessed when you're content with just who you are—no more, no less. That's the moment you find yourselves proud owners of everything that can't be bought." When are you most likely to be content with who you are? When are you least likely to be content with who you are? In your own words, how would you state the invitation of God in Jesus' words?

4

LETTING GO

SOME OF US ARE JUST BEGINNING to notice losses in our lives. Others have already noticed a plethora of losses that have accumulated over the years. *As we notice the losses, God invites us to let go.* Noticing the losses and letting go are different experiences. Losses happen to us and are often out of our control. Letting go involves the choices we make in response to the losses. God's invitations in the losses usually surprise us. God invites us to let go of things that no longer work for us, that no longer satisfy us, or that are no longer needed. Invitations to let go have been coming to us throughout our lives. But now, as we age, things change a bit. The need to let go of unused, misguided, worn-out ways of living seem to come more often. As we age, God invites us to release things we are losing anyway.

Even if we hear invitations in our losses and see the glimmers of hope in new ways of living, it will be hard to let go. Jesus told two short parables that apply to many stages of life but can be of special help to us as we navigate the experience of letting go in our senior years. In the first parable, Jesus said, "The kingdom of heaven is like treasure hidden in a field. When a man found it, he hid it again, and then in his joy went and sold all he had and bought that field." This must have been an important parable because Jesus quickly told another one which was very similar: "Again," Jesus said, "the kingdom of heaven is like a merchant looking for fine pearls. When he found one of great value, he went away and sold everything he had and bought it" (Matthew 13:44-46). We are like that man and that merchant. As we age, it may seem that we are asked to "sell" so much, but the truth is that when we let go, we are "purchasing" great treasures.

Jesus said that the man who bought the field went out in joy and sold all he had. The merchant who bought the pearl knew he had found just what he was looking for. Is it possible for us to let go of parts of our life *with joy*? Is it possible to see in the experience of old age things that we have actually been looking for? Yes, both things are possible, but each one requires that we "let go" of the familiar in order to "buy" something new.

RESISTANCE TO LETTING GO

The temptation is to resist letting go of what we have. Some of us resist giving up lifelong jobs. Others resist giving up their role in church. Others resist giving up the role they have had in their family. One size does not fit all. By the time we reach our senior years, we have found places where our God-given gifts are used in our jobs, in ministry, and in our families. But difficulty for each of us in letting go of our familiar roles in life is usually just the beginning. Unfortunately, the false self loves to hide in our giftedness. Probably unknown to us, the false self has convinced us that without our gifts, we are nothing. As we age, when we feel increasingly vulnerable, we may resist losing the roles and jobs that have allowed us to use our gifts, sometimes for good but sometimes to meet our ego demands.

It takes careful discernment to tell what is motivating us. Our gifts have helped us do our jobs well. God gave us our abilities and talents to bless us and to bless others. Most of us are very grateful for all that God has given us. But that does not stop us from using our gifts in self-serving ways. Underneath our resistance to change, we may see the pride of the false self. To be honest, I am thankful for the gifts God has given me to help me write, but I feel much better about myself if my books sell well. My pastor friends tell me that they feel better if the pews in church are full on Sunday mornings, even though their pastoral gifts come from God. My friends in business are happier when their income increases, even though they do not want to be materialistic. In other words, the false self deceives us, often allowing our gifts to become sources of pride and entitlement. As we age, our gifts may become overused and tarnished. The losses we experience as we age shatter the image the false self wants to project. This experience feels like a crash course in humility. In order to listen well to what God might be saying to us, we need self-awareness, discernment, and patience.

SELF-AWARENESS AS WE AGE

Choosing to be self-aware is often another experience of liminal space. Some people move into their senior years with vigorous, authentic self-awareness, but many people have never paid much attention to their inner life. Others consider it selfish to think about themselves. It helps to remember that self-awareness is a tool God gives us not only to help us know ourselves better but also to know God better. In fact, John Calvin said that we cannot know God unless we know ourselves. "Nearly all wisdom," he said, "consists of two parts: the knowledge of God and of ourselves. . . . The knowledge of ourselves not only arouses us to seek God, but also, as it were, leads us by the hand to find him."[1]

For those of us who might be uncertain about this, Scripture is full of reminders to pay attention to ourselves. The prophet Jeremiah said, "Let us examine our ways and test them" (Lamentations 3:40). The apostle Paul wrote, "Examine yourselves to see whether you are in the faith" (2 Corinthians 13:5). Most of us think of "examining ourselves" as a time to think about whether we have recently sinned. But theologians tell us it means much more. It means, as I understand it, to look at our lives and be sure we are still following in the ways God is leading us. Eugene Peterson translated Paul's words this way: "Test yourselves to make sure you are solid in the faith. Don't drift along taking everything for granted.

Give yourselves regular checkups. You need firsthand evidence, not mere hearsay, that Jesus Christ is in you" (2 Corinthians 13:5, MSG).

These verses are reminders for us as we age. We will not age well if we "drift along," assuming that life will not change. We need to keep paying attention to ourselves. When we listen carefully, we will hear the whispers of the Holy Spirit to our spirits, inviting us to grow and change. "Let's take a good look at the way we're living," Jeremiah says, "and reorder our lives under GOD" (Lamentations 3:40, MSG). Commenting on the aging experience, respected author Parker Palmer writes to all of us, "We need to reframe aging as a passage of discovery and engagement."[2] Reframing and reordering our lives as we grow older will require self-awareness that invites us to let go of the past and embrace our new life. But this is not easy.

One way we can reorder and reframe our lives is to reflect on ways that we have changed. God's love and grace never change, but we do. In many ways, we are the same people we were twenty or thirty years ago, but we are also very different. Our perspectives, desires, and values have been nuanced by our life experiences. This probably means we have thoughts that are new to us and desires that have expanded. We are beginning to let go of some of the things that were important to us in our earlier years. The way God invites me to let go is different from the way God invites my husband to let go and different from the way each of my older friends lets go. Letting go looks different in our sixties, seventies, and eighties. But God continually invites us to notice what is happening. We are invited to notice and reflect on our changing desires and motivations, as well as our changing thoughts and assumptions.

NOTICING THE CHANGING DESIRES OF OUR HEARTS

According to the psalmist David, God gives us "the desires of [our] heart[s]" (Psalm 37:4). It seems unlikely that David meant that God would give us everything we want, which was my youthful interpretation. Now, years later, I believe that this verse means that God plants desires in my heart. My desires may be stained by my own selfishness, but in their purest form, they are God-given. It is certainly true that out of grace, God does not give me everything I want. Some things I think I want are not good for me. Nevertheless, until I humbly listen well to my heart, I will not know God's desires for me. The desires God has given me help me know the desires God has for me. This is very good news! But it becomes complicated as we age, especially as we notice that our desires are changing.

The desires I brought into my own adult life began as soon as I graduated from college. I wanted to reach out to teach others about their faith. I joined a campus ministry, and I loved the one-on-one relationship with college students. Then, to my surprise, I found out that I also loved speaking to large groups. I had found my niche. As the college students grew up, I grew with them. Soon I was leading women's Bible studies and speaking to larger women's groups. I thought I would do this forever. I experienced joy every time I spoke to groups of women. I was doing what God wanted me to do.

When I was in my forties and my fifties, I was still speaking to women's groups. I loved the excitement of weekends away with women who wanted to grow in their faith. I loved being the one up front who was helping them. I loved, of course, the affirmation I received. But something was changing. I began to notice that my enthusiasm for speaking at conferences was waning. The weekends away began to seem repetitive. One friend told me that she loved going to conferences because, she said, "They pump me up." But I noticed that being "pumped up" didn't seem to last for many of the women. The desire of my heart to speak at conferences was changing direction. I wasn't sure if this was a good thing, but I knew I wanted to engage in something deeper, something, shall we say, with a longer shelf life. Then I discovered spiritual direction. I wondered if this intimate and personal ministry was a better fit for me than speaking to large groups.

About that time, I got a phone call that unsettled me in a very deep way. It turned out to be one of those midlife experiences that is now informing me in the process of aging. The director of women's ministry at a church in Alaska asked if I would be able to come to speak at the conference they were planning for the next fall. My heart sank. My gut clenched. I didn't want to go. What was wrong with me? Alaska is beautiful. I was honored by the invitation. But I was so tired, and my heart's desire was to stay home. This desire bumped headfirst into desires and values I had had all my adult life. Would I be letting God down if I gave in to my desire to turn down this request to speak? Admittedly, this was not the first time I had been reluctant about speaking, but it was the first time I allowed myself to listen to my reluctance. I couldn't say no, but I couldn't say yes. So I asked her to call me back in a few months. She never did. Looking back, I suspect that God was sparing me from having to say no. After all, I was just learning to listen to the changing desires of my heart.

NOTICING CHANGING ASSUMPTIONS AS WE AGE

One of the reasons noticing the desires of our hearts is a challenge is that our desires and our assumptions about ourselves and God are all intertwined. And by the time we reach our senior years, we are usually entrenched in familiar ways of thinking. I grew up as a Christian believing that serving God in my work was the way to live out my faith. As I aged, my diminishing energy and my changing desires threatened this belief I had lived with most of my life. I remember the first time it registered with me that Jesus actually said, "My yoke is easy and my burden is light" (Matthew 11:30). I said to myself, *I can only wish that were true!*

Slowly and gently, God invited me to question the assumptions behind my "holy service" for God. Slowly and gently, God invited me to believe that perhaps Jesus' yoke is indeed easy and light. Looking back, I can see that in my younger years, the "work" of speaking and teaching was usually a "light burden" that I carried easily. But as I grew older, the burden became heavier. I needed to pay attention to the weight I was feeling, and I needed to notice the assumptions and the thinking behind my resistance to change. It was important for me to see if the Holy Spirit was leading me into new truth (John 16:12).

This, too, was liminal space, but it was not as threatening as I first feared. My increasing awareness of God's love had softened some of the things that I assumed were true. I was coming to believe that God's love was not dependent on my works, or even my obedience. About this time, I rediscovered Ecclesiastes 7:16: "Do not be overrighteous, neither be overwise—why destroy yourself?" This verse had spoken to me in other seasons of my life, but I had forgotten about it. Now, on the cusp of old age, I wondered if perhaps I was being overrighteous in my service and work for God. And I was pretty sure I was destroying something in my experience of God's love and grace. Changing my mind about what I thought I should do "for God" was a new wineskin to contain the new wine in my aging soul.

This kind of change is difficult for me, but I am encouraged by the biblical account of how Peter, one of the first church leaders, changed his mind. His experience of letting go of a deeply held assumption about himself and God began when he fell asleep up on a rooftop near Joppa. This is how his experience is described in Acts 10:11-16.

> He saw heaven opened and something like a large sheet being let down to earth by its four corners. It contained all kinds of four-footed animals, as well as reptiles and birds. Then a voice told him, "Get up, Peter. Kill and eat."
>
> "Surely not, Lord!" Peter replied. "I have never eaten anything impure or unclean."
>
> The voice spoke to him a second time, "Do not call anything impure that God has made clean."
>
> This happened three times, and immediately the sheet was taken back to heaven.

In Peter's "dream" he responded as he probably would have when he was awake. He said, in effect, "Oh, no, I have never done anything like that. It would be wrong to do what you are suggesting." That sounds like me telling God that I cannot change my mind about something I have believed all my life. Thankfully, God often tells me the same thing over and over, as he did with Peter in the dream. When Peter finally listened to God and went into the home of a Gentile, his actions changed the history of the Christian church. When I allow God to change my mind, the change often transforms my own life.

Peter was probably much younger than me, but his experience of changing his mind reminds me of how attached I am to what I believe about God's expectations of me. My own spiritual journey has been full of assumptions about what it means to live my life faithfully. Now as I consider how to age faithfully, I notice that many of my familiar ways of looking at life have more to say about me than about God's love and grace. As I grow older, my aging body and my waning energy send me back to listen to the whispers of the Holy Spirit, to hear eternal truths in new ways.

THE DISCIPLINE OF IRRESPONSIBILITY
One area in my life where I am hearing new truth reflects my sense of personal responsibility in all walks

of life. Being overly responsible has been an issue for me for years. I thought I had resolved the problem years ago when I decided that I just needed to "keep going on when the going gets tough." How wrong I was! My compulsive responsibility and the reality of my life are shouting at me as I age.

I love helping people. I love solving problems. I love being seen as a responsible person. I have always been responsible—for myself, for others, for the world. I read the Bible to see what I should be doing. I listen to others to see what they need. I keep up with the news to see if there are any international responsibilities I need to attend to. I am, truthfully, rather proud of my ability to be responsible. Letting go of my assumptions about responsibility seems like a violation of my faith journey. And letting go means facing my fear that I might become a couch potato. It also means admitting the pride driving my choices about how to be responsible.

But now that my body is aging, I am getting very tired of the burden of my compulsive responsibility. My aging body is calling into question my familiar assumptions about the value I place on what I accomplish. Questioning these assumptions has led me to the throne of God in prayer. Sometimes when someone asks me to do something, I think, *There is no way I can do that!* Quietly and gently, God's Spirit often whispers to my spirit, *You don't have to do it all.* In all honesty, even standing at the throne of grace, I often resist, *Oh, God, you don't understand. I do have to do it all.*

Last summer, I decided to practice the "discipline of irresponsibility." (I made up that discipline under the prompting of the Holy Spirit.) I could see signs in my life of compulsively saying yes to requests for help. I admitted to myself that I was finding validation in being available to meet any need I sniffed out—in my family, my community, and my church. It was untenable for me to think of not being responsible. Who would I be if I didn't meet the needs I thought other people had? The Spirit suggested to me that I try.

I decided, with God's grace, that if a request came my way when I knew I was too tired to go, or too overloaded to find the brain space to respond, I would look at that overload as an invitation from God to say no to the request. I found out that this is very hard for me to do! It means that sometimes I am lying on the sofa reading a book when I should (in my mind) be out meeting a need. It means asking what will bring me health and peace rather than asking my default question: *What do I think needs to be done here?* Or the question I can hardly admit: *What can I do to impress God and other people?*

An amazing thing happened on the way to the sofa. I did not become a couch potato. Instead, I discovered that my compulsive need to be responsible is not always the word of the Lord, or even the expectations of those I loved. Through the discipline of irresponsibility, I discovered the joy of love. It was as though God had prepared loving things for me to do and I did them better after spending time on the sofa. Then I remembered that God had, in fact, prepared good works for me—good works for my young adult years, good works for midlife, and now good works for my senior years. "We are God's handiwork, created in Christ Jesus to do good works, which God prepared in advance for us to do" (Ephesians 2:10). When I compulsively rushed out to do whatever I thought "needed" to be done, or when I insisted that I should still do the good works of my younger years, I probably missed some of the works prepared for me.

It brings me joy that I am still growing. To me, that makes getting older worth the costs of aging.

HOW DO WE DECIDE?

Allowing ourselves to look at the changes we are experiencing raises some serious questions: What changes are good, what changes are misguided, and what changes might lead us to dishonor our faith?

Reflecting on these questions requires careful discernment. Discernment is important throughout our lives but especially in the conundrum of our senior years. We have a lifetime of deeply held priorities. We have learned to judge ourselves and others according to familiar standards. Now, as we age, we are changing. And we may compare ourselves to others who are changing in different ways from us. Like the disciple Peter, we may say of our friends, "Lord, what about him?" (John 21:21). Jesus might answer, as he did to Peter, "If I want him to remain alive until I return, what is that to you? You must follow me" (John 21:22). Yes, we must follow Jesus into our old age. But we will need help in discerning what that means.

Again, self-awareness is one of our tools. Self-awareness and discernment are undeniably linked together. Author Thomas Green wrote that "the greatest obstacle to real discernment . . . is not the intangible nature of God, but . . . our own lack of self-knowledge—even our *unwillingness* to know ourselves as we truly are."[3] And so we return to the value of paying attention to all that is happening in our bodies and souls. Fortunately, there is an ancient spiritual discipline to help us.

THE EXAMEN FOR DISCERNMENT

The Daily Examen is a discipline to help us in the process of discernment about our motivation and our life choices. The origins of this ancient practice go back to the teachings of Ignatius of Loyola, who taught that by examining ourselves daily, we can learn to distinguish between "consolation" and "desolation" in our lives. One interpretation of these unfamiliar terms is that consolations are the life-giving invitations of the Holy Spirit and desolations are the life-draining lies of the evil one. The Daily Examen helps us tell the difference between these two voices in our souls.

As with many of the ancient disciplines, I have found that I need to translate the teaching into my own vernacular in a way that is appropriate for me. My understanding of how to experience the discipline of the Daily Examen is to regularly set aside time (about ten minutes) to reflect on my life. As we think back over the events of the day (or even the week), we try to notice when we felt closest to God and when we felt most distant from God. We might also ask ourselves some of the questions suggested by Adele Calhoun in her *Spiritual Disciplines Handbook*:

For what moment today am I most grateful? For what moment today am I least grateful?

When did I give and receive the most love today? When did I give and receive the least love today?

Where was I aware of living out of the fruit of the Spirit? Where was there an absence of the fruit of the Spirit?[4]

Questions like these help us discern what perspectives, choices, and activities have led us into a deeper experience of God's presence, what has helped us love others more effectively, and what has brought us peace and joy. These insights help us discern how God's love and grace are leading us. God wants us to have peace. He wants to give us joy. The Daily Examen helps us notice when joy and peace happen.

Sometimes I look back on a longer period of time, and sometimes I muse ahead on the coming day. I may ask myself, looking back, *What things did I love doing in recent months? What things were draining for me?* Or looking ahead, I might ask, *What am I most looking forward to today? What am I looking forward to the least?* Personal reflections like this help us grow in our capacity to be aware of what we are experiencing and to better discern God's guidance. This is a gentle discipline that helps us pay attention to the wisdom the Spirit is giving us about ourselves and about God's ways in our own lives.

BEING PATIENT WITH OURSELVES

As we grow in self-awareness and in discernment, we will undoubtedly need to be patient with ourselves. I keep thinking that I will live happily ever after. That when I get really old, I will have learned everything I need to know. The truth is, I am still waiting. I am encouraged by the parable Jesus told:

> "The kingdom of heaven is like a man who
> sowed good seed in his field. But while
> everyone was sleeping, his enemy came and
> sowed weeds among the wheat, and went away.

When the wheat sprouted and formed heads, then the weeds also appeared.

The owner's servants came to him and said, 'Sir, didn't you sow good seed in your field? Where then did the weeds come from?'

'An enemy did this,' he replied.

The servants asked him, 'Do you want us to go and pull them up?'

'No,' he answered, 'because while you are pulling the weeds, you may uproot the wheat with them. Let both grow together until the harvest. At that time I will tell the harvesters: First collect the weeds and tie them in bundles to be burned; then gather the wheat and bring it into my barn.'"

MATTHEW 13:24-30

As with most stories, this one can be understood from different perspectives. The parable is often seen as a story to describe the cosmic reality of good and evil. Thomas Green, in *Weeds Among the Wheat*, suggests a more personal perspective. He observes that all of us experience good and evil within ourselves. Even the apostle Paul wrote, "when I want to do good, evil is right there with me" (Romans 7:21, NIrv). Green notes that the parable describes our own experiences as we move through life and struggle with the weeds within. He writes, "the mysterious fact is that it seems we must allow the weeds to grow until the harvest, lest 'when you pull out the weeds you might pull up the wheat with them.'"[5] Applying this to my own experience of aging, I am reminded of how the false self might influence me as I tend to the garden of my aging soul. The false self tells me that if I just clean things up, if I get rid of all the weeds, I will be perfectly aged. And so I am tempted to try to pull up all the weeds at once. Thank goodness God is more patient with us. Some days, we will see the weeds in our lives. But other days, we glimpse the harvest. Sometimes it is only with hindsight that we know the difference.

THE PARABLE OF A MIDLIFE CRISIS

Looking back over our life together, Bob and I often reflect on one season that was full of weeds and wheat. This difficult season has become a personal parable for us. In every life, parables happen. We may not call them parables at the time, but looking back, we can often see the same kinds of truth that Jesus described in his stories. Early in midlife, Bob and I experienced a parable in our marriage which was unexpected and, truth be told, one we did not want to hear. Now, as we are deep into the aging process, we can look back and see the beginnings of truths we were going to experience as we aged. We see in our own parable loss, letting go, and new birth.

Bob was essentially fired from the job he had loved for many years. Not exactly fired, but his supervisor said they were going to make some changes. "Bob, this is just a quarter turn. We still want you here, but your job will look different." Both Bob and I knew this was no quarter turn. Our life was changing. And, in fact, we ended up moving from our beloved home where we had raised our daughters to a city where I definitely did not want to go. Bob started a new job, still in ministry, but in a very different area of influence and expertise. I left my friends and my familiar haunts to start over again. When a longtime friend called several months after we moved and asked, "How does Bob like his new job?" I thought about all we had lost and replied with a sarcastic chip on my shoulder, "He loves it, and it's a good thing!"

Yes. It was a good thing. But I didn't know how good it was when I responded to our friend with a smirk in my voice. I was still digesting our difficult year. Now, with the benefit of hindsight, I can see several parts of the experience that blindsided us. First came the shock: How could God ask Bob to let go of the job he loved, the home he loved, and the expectations he had for himself and our life together? Then came anger, tears, and fear of the future. In the middle of the mess came God's prompting to forgive and to let go. Eventually Bob came to accept that life as he knew it was changing. The grace of Bob's acceptance was followed by the huge question: What would he do now?

As with many of Jesus' parables, Bob's midlife crisis was full of questions. Our losses and letting go often intersect in mystery. If we had listened carefully, we might have heard the Spirit whisper to us God's words to his people in exile: "'For I know the plans I have for you,' declares the LORD, 'plans to prosper you and not to harm you, plans to give you hope and a future'" (Jeremiah 29:11). But we were too busy putting our house on the market, packing up everything we owned, and saying our good-byes to think about this promise. Looking back, we see the hand of God. Through Bob's unchosen, undesired professional loss, we entered a new season of life that was more enriching for both of us than any previous season. That painful time of letting go has become a parable of God's love and of new life.

When Bob retired, years later, we made plans to move to be closer to our daughter and grandchildren. As with our move years before, this move was painful. It was hard work and full of losses, but we remembered from our midlife parable that there would be gifts and invitations even in the losses. Our younger years are teaching us as we enter the season of retirement and adjustment to senior living. The parable of Bob's midlife crisis is still speaking to us.

THE FREEDOM OF LETTING GO

Letting go is a daily invitation for those of us in our senior years. But letting go does not mean we no longer care about the very things we are trying to release. Letting go does not mean we say to ourselves or others "it doesn't matter anymore." Letting go, rather, means we are no longer compulsively attached to our old perspectives, hopes, and expectations. This is a kind of "indifference" that gives us freedom. Spiritual director and author Phileena Heuertz writes that "indifference or non-attachment means to live with interior freedom, letting nothing own us but love."[6]

As we grow older and experiment with letting go, we find freedom we have not had before. Jesus said, "The truth will set you free" (John 8:32). Paul wrote that "where the Spirit of the Lord is, there is freedom" (2 Corinthians 3:17). As we age, we are challenged by the truth in each loss. As these accumulated truths set us free, we can expect that letting go will bring ongoing freedom. This feels like putting down burdens we have carried all our lives.

The prophet Isaiah describes the burdens carried by those in Babylonia. He wrote that Bel and Nebo (Babylonian gods) were stooped low, bowed down by their idols. "The images that are carried about," he wrote, "are burdensome, a burden for the weary." Our own gods have different names: accomplishment, talent, good looks, efficiency, endless energy, money, even spiritual achievements. These are idols we carry about. They are burdensome and wearying. As we age, they are too much for us. God invites us to put them down. "Listen to me," God says, "you whom I have upheld since your birth, and have carried since you were born. Even to your old age and gray hairs I am he, I am he who will sustain you. I have made you and I will carry you; I will sustain you and I will rescue you" (Isaiah 46:1-4).

May God give us the grace to let go, put down our burdens, and be carried by his love.

QUESTIONS FOR REFLECTION AND DISCUSSION

1. Is self-awareness something that comes easily to you, or is it something that is difficult? In what ways would you like to be more self-aware? How does self-awareness help you in your relationship with God?

2. What is your perspective on the "desires of your heart" (Psalm 37:4)? When have you followed your desires in life-giving ways?

3. What do you like about the Daily Examen? What about it sounds hard for you? What have been your experiences with this kind of reflection?

A PERSONAL MEDITATION: LETTING GO

1. Spend a few minutes practicing the discipline suggested by the Examen as you reflect on your younger years. Try to remember a particular season of life, and answer the following questions.

- When did you feel closest to God in that season? What were you doing when you felt the most freedom? What were you doing when you felt the most grateful?
- When did you feel most distant from God? What did you do that was most discouraging for you? What do you most regret about the season you are remembering?
- What is God's invitation to you in these reflections?

2. Consider your life now, as you are aging, in light of Galatians 6:4-5, translated in *The Message*:

> Make a careful exploration of who you are and the work you have been given, and then sink yourself into that. Don't be impressed with yourself. Don't compare yourself with others. Each of you must take responsibility for doing the creative best you can with your own life.

- How is the work you have been given to do different now than it was a few years ago?

- When are you most likely to be impressed with yourself?
- When are you most likely to compare yourself with others?
- What comes to mind when you think of taking "responsibility for doing the creative best" with your life today?

5

FEAR AND PEACE

SEVERAL YEARS AGO, when I was still in my young sixties, an older woman approached me after I spoke at a
church gathering. She must have been ninety years old,
with white hair and a curved spine. She looked up at
me and said, "I am just so scared." I was much younger
than she was and I didn't understand. The talk I had
just given was not about aging. Looking back, I can see
that she wasn't looking for a reason why she didn't need
to be afraid. She was more likely longing for someone
to love her in the midst of her fear. I was busy balancing
my coffee cup and catching my breath from giving a
talk I barely remember now. I also don't remember the

rest of my conversation with this very honest woman. But I have wondered about her since then. How did God help her in her fear? Was she able to draw close to God's love and grace? And did she see love in my eyes, even though I did not know how to respond to her?

Now I know that this ninety-year-old friend was brave enough to express what most of us keep hidden: As we age, we come face-to-face with fear in a way most of us have not known before. We have all been afraid at some of the milestones in our lives. I was afraid the first day I went to school, afraid when I started my first job, and afraid when we took our daughters to college. I faced new fears recently when we moved a thousand miles across the country at the same time we were advancing into the eighth decade of our lives. Even though fear is a familiar companion, for most people I know, fears multiply and intensify as we get older. We fear experiencing more and more losses. We may fear illness or financial loss. We probably fear becoming vulnerable. Fear is very personal, and we experience it in unique and intimate ways. The learning curve is steep as we age.

How can we live well with our fears? We cannot ignore them. Usually we cannot solve the problems behind them. But our lives do not need to be fear driven. In fact, Scripture says that "perfect love drives out fear" (1 John 4:18). This verse is a reminder that God's love can remove the fear of punishment and judgment after death. But could it also speak to our fears this side of death? The translation in *The Message* indicates that it does: "There is no room in love for fear. Well-formed love banishes fear. Since fear is crippling, a fearful life—fear of death, fear of judgment—is one not yet fully formed in love" (1 John 4:18, MSG). Here again, then, we see an area of growth in our old age. As we notice and respond to our fears, God extends mercy and grace and offers to transform our lives from lives of fear to lives of peace. Jesus said, as he wept over Jerusalem, "I wish you had known today what would bring you peace!" (Luke 19:42, NIrv). We are invited, as we age, to learn what will bring us peace in this always-new season of life.

TRANSFORMATION OF FEAR INTO PEACE

Zechariah, father of John the Baptist, reminds us that God will guide us into peace.

> Through the heartfelt mercies of our God,
> God's Sunrise will break in upon us,

Shining on those in the darkness,
    those sitting in the shadow of death,
Then showing us the way, one foot at a time,
    down the path of peace.

LUKE 1:79, MSG

What a gift this promise is. God will show us the way, one footstep at a time, down the path of peace. As we walk this path, we see several milestones along the way. First of all, we may notice that peace is a fruit of the Holy Spirit in our lives, along with a number of other good things like love, patience, kindness, and joy—things we long for at any age (Galatians 5:22-23). We have the advantage that by our old age, we have experienced these fruits of the Spirit in many different ways during our lifetimes. We also have the bitter-sweet advantage of remembering many times when we did not live in ways that expressed those fruits. As we reflect on those difficult times, we can be thankful that Jesus said God is like a gardener. Jesus taught that every branch that bears fruit, he trims "so that it will be even more fruitful" (John 15:2). By the time we reach our senior years, we have been trimmed many times. Some branches in our lives have even been thrown away. We still have more leaves and branches to trim, but perhaps learning to notice our losses and letting go of the dead branches will help us be more fruitful. Perhaps the fruit of peace will blossom as we age.

On the path of peace, we can also remember that peace is a gift. Jesus said, "Peace I leave with you; my peace I give you" (John 14:27). Because peace is a fruit of the Holy Spirit and peace is something given to us, we do not need to strive for it, try to make it happen, or even understand where it comes from. It is given to us. It almost seems to have a life of its own, apart from our understanding or our circumstances. Paul prayed that "the peace of God, which transcends all understanding," will guard our hearts and minds (Philippians 4:7). We can't understand the peace we experience because, as Jesus said, this peace is not the same as what the world offers (John 14:27). It is not a pretend peace we have generated, or a peace that comes from a reversal of our losses, or even a peace that comes from a good medical diagnosis. It is something wonderfully and mysteriously different from what we can understand or explain.

Jesus also said, "I have told you these things, so that in me you may have peace. In this world you will have trouble. But take heart! I have overcome the world" and

"Do not let your hearts be troubled and do not be afraid" (John 16:33; 14:27). *The Message* says that Jesus invites us to be "deeply at peace" (John 16:33, MSG). As we continue to age, we are invited to accept the deep peace Jesus offers. We will see this peace touch our lives as we experience some of the new fears of old age: the fear of uselessness, the fear of loneliness, the fear of our own brokenness, and the fear of death. We can learn to walk down the path of peace even amid our fears.

PEACE IN USELESSNESS

One disturbing fear we face in aging is a sense of uselessness. I can hardly think of a greater insult than to say of someone, "He is so useless!" And yet, as we age, we let go of many useful things we did in our younger years. We may fear that we have entered a season of nonproductivity, incompetence, or, as one friend said, "creeping irrelevancy." We are not useful to our families or our society in the ways we used to be. God is waiting to transform us and teach us to love others in smaller, unseen ways.

John writes in his letter to the early church, "no one has ever seen God; but if we love one another, God lives in us and his love is made complete in us" (1 John

4:12). Paul said something very similar. "In my flesh," he wrote, "I am completing what is lacking in Christ's afflictions for the sake of his body, that is, the church" (Colossians 1:24, NRSV). Jesus hinted at this when he told his disciples that they would do "even greater" works than he was doing because he was "going to the Father" (John 14:12). Are John and Paul and Jesus saying that Jesus' works on earth and death on the cross were incomplete? I can hardly believe that! But it is true. God continues the work of divine love through us. We complete what Jesus began. Amazing! Our work of completion, making up for what is lacking, and doing greater works than Jesus, continues even in our old age. We may fear we won't be as useful, but we do not need to fear that we can no longer love. In this season of life, we are called to love in new ways.

I have a black-and-white photo of my grandmother sitting with me on our front porch when I was about two years old. She is looking at me with radiant joy. Love and kindness are so evident in her face that as I look at the picture, I know I must have felt loved. I didn't know then that God's love for me was being made complete in my grandmother's love. But now I can see that. And now, I am the grandma. Sometimes

I am an active participant in life, but often I am quiet when the rest of the family is running around. I watch my grandchildren, engage in conversations with them, pray for them, and am simply present in their lives. In this quiet, nonactive participation, God's love is being made complete in me. This is a miracle of old age. It is so different from what I used to do, but I thank God that he is still completing his love for others through me. It is the gift of my age to those around me.

When we sit down, do less, and listen well, we may feel useless, but it is a "uselessness" full of grace, love, and peace.

PEACE IN LONELINESS

Another fear most of us experience, even those of us who like to be alone, is the fear of loneliness. We fear social isolation. We fear being misunderstood by those we love. We fear facing pain alone. We even fear spiritual loneliness. Loneliness is not just a symptom of old age. It is epidemic in our society. My friend Claire is a psychotherapist with a large clientele. She tells me that loneliness is the number-one issue she hears about from her clients. In fact, her clients often tell her that she is the only one they can talk to who listens. I asked her how she listens. She said, "I ask questions." Most of us do not want answers and solutions. We want someone to be interested in who we are.

As we age, our fear of loneliness, like all our fears, may become greater, but it also has the potential to lead us into a deeper experience of God's presence. Scripture teaches that we experience God's love through other people. Paul hints at this when he says that we "comfort those in any trouble with the comfort we ourselves receive from God" (2 Corinthians 1:4). By the time we reach our senior years, we have probably comforted many people. Now is the time for us to receive comfort from others. When we take the risk of reaching out to others and sharing ourselves with them, we learn to experience God's love through them. We can ask God for the courage to be honest about what we fear. We can ask for the humility to reach out for help and understanding. God is "the Father of compassion and the God of all comfort, who comforts us in all our troubles" (2 Corinthians 1:3-4). As we ask God for his comfort, we may find it comes enfleshed in other people. God may give us companions on the journey, friends, family members, spiritual directors, and pastors who have not yet experienced all of our fears, but as they listen to us, God will be present in them and whisper his peace to our spirits. It takes courage to admit our losses and our fears, but sharing our lives and our concerns with others is an important way to accept the peace God wants to give us.

PEACE IN OUR BROKENNESS

By the time we reach our senior years, we all have broken pieces in our lives. I am sad about my own broken pieces. I still feel the weight of leftover, unresolved depression. On some days, my self-judgment is much stronger than my confidence in divine grace. And on other days, my pride shouts out at me, even though I should know not to listen to my false self. I live with the regret that my relationship with my parents never fully reflected God's love. I regret some things I have done, and I regret some things I have not done. The truth is, no matter what our age, we still fall short. Our church liturgy reads, "Holy God, forgive us our sins: what we have done and what we have left undone. We have failed to love others and failed to love you with our whole selves." Every Sunday, I need to pray that prayer.

Parker Palmer, in his book on *Grace, Gravity and Getting Old*, reassures those of us who struggle with this sense of brokenness:

Wholeness is the goal, but wholeness does not mean perfection. It means embracing brokenness as an integral part of life. The sooner we understand this, the better. It's a truth that can set us free to live well, to love well, and, in the end, to die well.[1]

Fortunately, God is not surprised by our brokenness. The Bible reminds us that we are like clay pots. The prophet Isaiah wrote: "You, LORD, are our Father. We are the clay, you are the potter; we are all the work of your hand" (Isaiah 64:8). The problem is that pots can break. My friend Tom told me, "I am terrified that the brokenness of my life will invalidate my ministry." The brokenness he feels weighs on him as he begins to process what it means to grow older. It is a heavy burden for him to bear.

We can be encouraged by a vision of Jeremiah. "I went down to the potter's house," he said, "and I saw him working at the wheel. But the pot he was shaping from the clay was marred in his hands; so the potter formed it into another pot, shaping it as seemed best to him" (Jeremiah 18:3-4). God has been reshaping us most of our lives. One way to look at the aging experience is to remember that God is still reshaping us. Perhaps there is still hope. I can almost picture myself standing before my heavenly Father with a handful of broken pieces. I might say, *I am so, so sorry. The potter did a good job. But I dropped the pot. And now I can't get these pieces back together. Please help me!*

The Japanese art of kintsugi gives me a hint of how God might respond to my request. In kintsugi, artists use gold, silver, and platinum to "glue" the broken pieces of pottery together. The art form originated in the fifteenth century in attempts to fix broken tea bowls and other ordinary ceramic items. Today kintsugi artists take broken pieces and make them more beautiful than ever before. They are also considered much, much more valuable than they were in their original form. Remembering this in light of our own lives can bring us peace. God is a potter, and God is an artist. Even our broken pieces can be made into something new. In our old age, God may make us even more beautiful.

PEACE IN OUR LAST SEASON

As we navigate each season of the aging process, we all know that one of these seasons will be our last. Most of us are afraid to talk about death, especially our own.

Talking about death is probably the last frontier in our efforts to be honest and authentic. In our society, people are freer to talk about addictions and sex than to talk about dying. Perhaps this is because death is the final proof that we are not in control. It is humbling to admit to our fear of dying. And yet Scripture never shies away from this topic we avoid. The psalmist reminds us to "number our days, that we may gain a heart of wisdom" (Psalm 90:12). In other words, remembering that we are going to die gives us wisdom.

Jesus did not hesitate to talk about his own death. In fact, he insisted on talking about it. When he spoke publicly about his upcoming death, Peter rebuked him in private. Jesus responded, "You do not have in mind the concerns of God, but merely human concerns" (Mark 8:33). On another occasion, when he spoke of his death again, his disciples "did not understand what he meant and were afraid to ask him about it" (Mark 9:32). Apparently we are not the only ones afraid to talk about death. When they followed Jesus up to Jerusalem and he spoke about his death again, Mark tells us that the disciples were "astonished" and others who followed were "afraid" (Mark 10:32).

The apostle Paul spoke freely about death. In fact,

he indicated that in our life of faith, we "carry around in our body the death of Jesus, so that the life of Jesus may also be revealed in our body" (2 Corinthians 4:10). How we can be alive *and* have experienced death is a great mystery of faith. Speaker and author Richard Rohr touched on this when he wrote:

> In the larger-than-life, spiritually transformed people I have met, I always find one common denominator: in some sense, they have all died before they died. They have followed in the self-emptying steps of Jesus, a path from death to life that Christians from all over the world celebrate [at Easter].[2]

Death, then, is not a subject to avoid. We do not need to be embarrassed or ashamed by our fear of death. God invites us to raise questions about all the fears we have, including those we have as we face this last stage of our journey. David Steindl-Rast, in his book on gratefulness, says that "to prevent questions from weighing us down we must raise them."[3] Thomas, the disciple always brave enough to ask questions, asked Jesus what he meant when he promised life after death. Thomas said, "Lord, we don't know where you are going, so how can we know the way?" (John 14:5). We might ask the same question at this point in our lives. How are we supposed to know the way we are going? How can we navigate well the way to death? We might also admit that sometimes it is not so much the grave we fear as the route that will take us there. Personally I'm not at all sure I like thinking about the route to death. Sometimes the terrain and the scenery look frightening.

Fear like this probably seems theoretical to those who are just on the brink of old age. It is hard to imagine what it will be like to experience our last years. But we can catch glimpses of the fears to come. I am writing during the COVID-19 pandemic. Many people have commented that this pandemic has reminded them of their own mortality. We are reminded that we will not live forever. We are not immune to disease or to tragedy. We want to be more entitled than pandemics allow, to be more knowledgeable, and to be more in control. This pandemic is causing young and old people alike to think about their fears. It is also a vivid reminder to those of us in our senior years of the fears to come as we age. Thankfully, there is a spiritual discipline which may help us find peace in the midst of our anxiety.

PEACE IN SILENCE

The discipline of "silence and solitude" is getting a lot of attention these days. Blogs, retreats, and books teach us and invite us to experience the gifts of this discipline. Most of the teaching, I've noticed, is directed toward active, busy midlifers. When we age, our bodies slow us down. Hopefully, as we have embraced the process of aging, we have learned much about the gifts of being still and being quiet in the presence of God. But as in all seasons of life, we need reminders about this counter-cultural experience. How can we experience silence and solitude in life-giving ways when we are old? How might this discipline help us find peace in the midst of our fears?

A good place to start is Psalm 46. From this psalm we learn that "God is our refuge and strength, an ever-present help in trouble. Therefore we will not fear, though the earth give way and the mountains fall into the heart of the sea" (Psalm 46:1-2). That sounds pretty scary to me. What if our backyard collapses and the Rocky Mountains fall into the lake down the street? How could I "not fear" if that ever happens? What would God say to me then? He would say, according to Psalm 46:10, "Alice, be still!" In light of my imagined disaster, this advice seems strange. Why would being "still" help in that situation?

In the face of our real fears of aging, when life is changing, collapsing, and falling apart, why would God say to us "Be still"? But this is God's invitation to us. Blaise Pascal, mathematician, scientist, writer, and theologian of the seventeenth century, wrote, "I have discovered that all the unhappiness of men arises from one single fact, that they cannot stay quietly in their own room."[4] If this is true, then those of us in our old age have an advantage. We are in a season of life where sitting quietly is becoming more normal. In fact, the practice of silence and solitude is a bit easier for me now than it was in the driven, busy life of my younger years. But I still need encouragement to practice the discipline suggested in Psalm 46, the discipline of being still and knowing that God is God.

Being still for me means accepting the opportunity to spend time alone, in quiet, without an agenda. I just sit. I don't try to solve problems, though sometimes that happens. I don't think of a lot of suggestions I would like to give to God about my own life, my family, or the world. I breathe deeply. Sometimes I have a sense that God is breathing prayers within me. Sometimes I look out the window at nature declaring the glory of God. Sometimes I do nothing.

But usually out of that stillness, I "know" that God is. Sometimes Scripture comes to mind reminding me of who God is. Sometimes I remember that God is still healing places in my life that are weighing on my soul. But sometimes I don't really think at all. I just know that God is with me, even though I do not understand all that I know. And sometimes I just sit in the peacefulness of those moments. This is another gift of old age.

God says to us all, "Be still and know that I am God." There are so many things we do not know as we age. We do not know when we will die. We do not know why God allowed us to lose so much that is important to us. We do not know if we can live out the life that has been given to us. Some days all we do know is that God is God. God created us, and God loves us. "The Lord Almighty is with us" (Psalm 46:11). We accept peace when we are still and silent enough to remember that.

GOD IS PRAYING FOR US

We can also remember that the Holy Spirit is our companion as we sit in silence. Even more amazing, the

Holy Spirit is praying for us. Paul wrote to the Romans, "the Spirit helps us in our weakness. We do not know what we ought to pray for, but the Spirit himself intercedes for us through wordless groans" (Romans 8:26). In our silence, we can be at peace, knowing that the Spirit is praying for us. And what a comfort it is to know that the prayers of the Spirit are "in accordance with the will of God" (Romans 8:27). This takes the burden off our shoulders to pray for just the right outcomes of our fears.

Earlier in his letter to the Roman church, Paul offered words of comfort that reflect Jesus' words about new birth. Paul said that "the whole creation has been groaning as in the pains of childbirth . . . We ourselves . . . groan inwardly as we wait eagerly for our adoption . . . the redemption of our bodies" (Romans 8:22-23). God hears the cries of our old age. It is comforting to me to know that I am once again in the "pains of childbirth." Six decades ago, I was "born again." Now, I am experiencing a new birth in another way. Paul writes: "The difficult times of pain throughout the world are simply birth pangs. But it's not only around us; it's *within* us. The Spirit of God is arousing us within. We're also feeling the birth pangs. These sterile and barren bodies of ours are yearning for full deliverance" (Romans 8:22-23, MSG).

And so the birth image helps me again as it did at the beginning of my journey. God is always the Life Giver. It is God's plan of grace and love to give new birth even at the end of our lives. Aging is the process of waiting for this final birth. "If we hope for what we do not yet have, we wait for it patiently" (Romans 8:25). "Meanwhile," Paul says, "the moment we get tired in the waiting, God's Spirit is right alongside helping us along" (Romans 8:26, MSG).

God wants to give us peace and patience as we wait. This is the holy invitation to all of us as we pursue spiritual transformation on the journey of aging.

QUESTIONS FOR REFLECTION AND DISCUSSION

1. To what extent do you relate to the fear of being useless? How do you respond to this fear?

2. When are you most likely to feel lonely? What do you do when you experience loneliness?

3. How does the weight of your own human brokenness affect you? What helps you with your regrets?

4. What is it like for you to have times of silence and solitude? Do you like times like that, or do you find them stressful? In what ways is being silent helpful to you?

5. How do you know when you are at peace?

FOR PERSONAL MEDITATION: FEAR AND PEACE

1. A quick Google search for "kintsugi pottery" comes up with lovely pictures of some of these pieces. Spend some time looking at these pieces of art and imagining God re-creating your own life in ways that put together the broken pieces with the gold and silver of his grace. What would you like your new pot to look like?

   • Put your thoughts into a prayer offered to the Divine Potter.

2. Look at Paul's words from Romans 8 and underline the ones that stand out to you today.

> All around us we observe a pregnant creation. The difficult times of pain

throughout the world are simply birth pangs. But it's not only around us; it's *within* us. The Spirit of God is arousing us within. We're also feeling the birth pangs. These sterile and barren bodies of ours are yearning for full deliverance. That is why waiting does not diminish us, any more than waiting diminishes a pregnant mother. We are enlarged in the waiting. We, of course, don't see what is enlarging us. But the longer we wait, the larger we become, and the more joyful our expectancy.

Meanwhile, the moment we get tired in the waiting, God's Spirit is right alongside helping us along. If we don't know how or what to pray, it doesn't matter. He does our praying in and for us, making prayer out of our wordless sighs, our aching groans. He knows us far better than we know ourselves, knows our pregnant condition, and keeps us present before God. That's why we can be so sure that every detail in our lives of love for God is worked into something good.

ROMANS 8:22-28, MSG

- Write another prayer telling the Divine Midwife how you feel about the words you underlined.

3. In the midst of the Holocaust, Dutch author Etty Hillesum had this to say about peace:

> Ultimately, we have just one moral duty: to reclaim large areas of peace in ourselves, more and more peace, and to reflect it toward others. And the more peace there is in us, the more peace there will also be in our troubled world.[5]

- What comes to mind when you think about reclaiming large areas of peace in your own life in this season of aging? How might you do that? And how might your peace be a gift to others?

Epilogue

Listening Well to Aging Friends

THE EPILOGUE OF A NOVEL often tells the reader what happened a few years after the story ends. The hero and heroine move to a new country, have four or five happy children, and live long and good lives. Our own lives are not so simple. As we age, we pass milestones along the way, but this side of heaven we never make the epilogical leap to living "happily ever after." We need loving companions to help us navigate each season of the aging process, with its liminal spaces, its rough spots, and its challenging choices.

This is a different kind of companionship from social interactions, which are also very important. But this kind of intentionally spiritual companionship can be a lifeline for those we love as they age. It can come in the form of friendship, family relationships, spiritual direction, or pastoral care. For those who are too young to have experienced the pitfalls of aging, it may seem like a daunting task to offer this kind of companionship. And for those of us who are already older and still facing the pitfalls ourselves, it may seem daunting for different reasons. But all of us, young and old alike, can grow in our ability to offer loving, spiritual listening.

I have been a spiritual director for about twenty-five years. When I meet with people, I do not give them answers or direction from my perspective. I want to help them hear the direction of God in their own lives. I do this mostly by asking questions and listening to them talk about themselves. I have met with young adults, people in midlife, and folks entering the experience of old age. I notice again and again, in young and old alike, that everyone wants to *be known*. Psychiatrist and author Curt Thompson writes, "Our Western world has long emphasized knowledge—factual information . . . — over the process of being known by God and others."[1] Being known opens the door to being loved. "It is love," Thompson says, "that transforms our minds."[2]

The Bible, in the classic chapter about love, says this:

When I was a child, I talked like a child, I
thought like a child, I reasoned like a child.
When I became a man, I put the ways of
childhood behind me. For now we see only a
reflection as in a mirror; then we shall see face
to face. Now I know in part; then I shall know
fully, even as I am fully known.

I CORINTHIANS 13:11-12

As we companion older people, it is good to remember that an older person no longer thinks like a child, but they still do not see themselves or God clearly. They may feel like they are "squinting in a fog," longing for the time when they will "see it all . . . see it all as clearly as God sees us, knowing him directly just as he knows us!" (1 Corinthians 13:12, MSG). As they wait for that time of being fully known, we can offer them loving companionship when we listen well, perhaps giving hints of how much God knows them and loves them.

HOW TO LISTEN WELL

Those who listen well listen without agenda, not trying to fix the problems that come with old age. They pay careful attention to what they hear, learning to say, "Tell me more about this experience you are having." "How do you feel about this?" "How is this different from what you used to experience?" Whatever questions they ask, they communicate that they want to be present. They want to support the older person they love. They do not want to change them. They just want to *be with* them. That kind of attentive listening reflects the patience and grace of God. It also decreases anxiety, gives emotional connection, and offers peace to the one listened to.

My sense about how to listen to those who are in the process of aging is that older people (actually, all people) want to be understood, rather than seen as a problem to be solved. They do not want to be talked out of their pain and sadness. They want to be believed and accepted as they are. Our aging friends are always in liminal space. They are getting older every day. Sometimes they need others to listen as they try to put into words all that is new to them. Those who listen well learn to listen without judgment. They listen with curiosity and openness. They try to listen with a welcoming demeanor that encourages the one they are companioning to talk about what is going on inside their souls. In this way, they invite them to age faithfully in love and grace.

SEASONS OF AGING

As we reach out to our older friends to offer intentional spiritual companionship, we will want to remember: People move in and out of the many parts of the aging process. We age differently at different times. I have come up with a list of questions that may be appropriate during the three most common decades of aging. My list is informed by my spiritual-direction perspective, but I hope it provides a starting place for anyone—sons and daughters, pastors and friends—who wants to offer loving, transformational companionship to those who are aging, one season at a time.

1. People in their sixties usually look at "old age" as something in the future. Sometimes they can hardly believe this will happen to them. But in their more honest moments, they begin to think ahead to the next season of life. They have probably spent much of their adult life preparing for the future: making professional plans, helping their children and others get ready for each season of life, and serving in the church to help set up future ministries. The spiritual challenge of planning for their own senior years is that there are so many unknowns. *What will my health be like as I age? What will the economy be doing when I get old? What will I do with myself when I retire?* These questions usually lie on top of deeper questions unique to each person. As we seek to provide spiritual companionship to those we love, we may be able to ask about the deeper questions. At their best, our questions are invitational, not trying to lead them to what we think they "should" think. We invite those we love to discover their own answers to the questions they may not have even known they were asking. Here are a few questions I might ask someone on the brink of their senior years:

- What are the biggest unknowns for you as you look ahead to your own aging experience?
- What things have been most life-giving for you so far in your life?
- What are your fears about getting older?
- What things are most important to you about your quality of life as you age?
- What comes to mind about how you would like to grow spiritually as you get older?

2. As people move into their seventies, they often come face-to-face with the realities of retirement, diminishing energy, and disappointing bodies. This is a life they have never lived before. As we companion people in this season, we will need to listen very carefully, not judgmentally, and with an ear to what they are *not* saying, even to themselves. We might ask them:

- What are some of the things that have surprised you about your retirement? What do you like about it? What do you not like about it?
- How are you responding to the physical changes in your body and your energy level?
- What unexpected parts of aging are you experiencing now?
- How has aging changed your relationship with your family? With God?
- Knowing what you know now about aging, how would you like to live as this process continues?

3. By the time people are in their eighties, medical issues have usually become an important part of life. Whether it is the onset of an illness or body parts that aren't working well, most people in their eighties find themselves needing medical help. Older people and their younger companions need help in navigating this time of life. The best guide I know is Dr. Atul Gawande, author of *Being Mortal.* Dr. Gawande writes as a compassionate physician, a respected surgeon, and a loving son to aging parents. We can learn much from the way he companioned his own parents in their senior years and how he continues to care for his patients.

He reminds his readers of the importance of talking about end-of-life questions. He suggests we ask the questions typically asked of older people who are entering the hospital or a nursing facility. These include questions about resuscitation, aggressive treatments, antibiotics, and feeding tubes. Of special interest to me, he notes that it is the *discussion*, not the list of questions, which "matter most." He said that when patients were offered discussions like this "they lived 25 percent longer."[3] Dr. Gawande asked his own father questions suggested by a palliative medical expert. When his father was facing paralysis, Gawande asked him about his fears if that should happen. He also asked what his goals were if his condition worsened. And he asked what trade-off he was willing to make and not willing to make to try to stop what was happening to him. Gawande said, "Those questions were among the hardest I'd asked in my life. . . . But what we felt afterward was relief. We felt clarity."[4] Being willing to take the risk of asking hard questions like this is a gift we can give to those we love.

It does not escape my notice that the kinds of discussions Dr. Gawande suggests for doctors relating to their patients include the same kind of attentiveness and respect that I learned about in my spiritual-direction training. As a doctor, he knew the importance of listening to the deepest desires of his patients. These desires informed the discernment process for moving forward medically. *What do you fear the most? What do you want the most? What will be most helpful to you as you experience this difficult event?* These types of questions are fodder for spiritual direction inside or outside of medical experiences.

Most people who companion older loved ones will not be doctors or spiritual directors. But they can still be loving listeners. In fact, this may be their calling for a season of life, as those they love need their spiritual companionship. My friend Margaret told me that she came to believe that caring for her mother was a "sacred assignment." She had not always had an easy relationship with her mother. But as her mother aged and faced serious medical complications, Margaret wanted to care for her vulnerabilities with "the same gentle presence that Jesus would want us to have for a vulnerable child." Margaret prayed that God would help her be patient. "I found," she said, "that empathy and encouragement helped calm her." Instead of trying to explain away what was happening in her mother's life, she would say, "I know, Mom. This has to be so hard for you. I can't imagine how I'd feel in your shoes." This kind of understanding and respect helped her mother gradually accept the unacceptable. "The last year and a half of Mom's earthly life," Margaret said, "revealed the beauty of her intimacy with Jesus."

In their eighties and beyond, then, our older friends and family members will need doctors and nurses, but they will also need to be surrounded by those who will listen with compassion and love. Love, the apostle Paul tells us, "bears all things, believes all things, hopes all things, endures all things" (1 Corinthians 13:7, NRSV). May God give us the grace to companion others with this kind of love. May we love them well in the last season of their lives.

Acknowledgments

I want to say a special thank-you to Dave Zimmerman, my friend and my editor at NavPress. Dave is gifted, attentive, understanding, and always helpful. He was like an editorial spiritual director, helping me discover what was already inside of me and then guiding me as I gave those perspectives new life. Dave, I am so very grateful.

Dave was joined by a fantastic team of people at NavPress and Tyndale House. They generously shared their own gifts (ones that I don't have!) to make this book all that it is. Thank you.

The first seeds for *Aging Faithfully* were planted over coffee by my friend, Arlene Bowie. She very persistently challenged my stubborn conclusion that I was too old to write another book. Thank you, Arlene. I was a slow learner, but I'm glad I listened to you.

Then there are the many friends who shared their own experiences about getting older. We talked over dinners, at our house and yours. We emailed. You answered my many questions. You deepened my understanding of the variety of ways there are to age faithfully. You are anonymous in the book but not in my gratitude.

And, of course, my thanks to my family: To my daughters, Dorie and Elisa, who have listened for years as I have processed my own journey into my senior years. To my granddaughter, Elizabeth, who puts up with me when I get tired—and when I can't hear what she just said. And to my husband, Bob, who has taken this journey alongside me. Thank you for growing old with me!

Appendix 1

Scripture about Life after Death

WE DON'T KNOW THE DETAILS of the years before our death, but God reassures us that he will guide us even beyond the epilogue of our lives. We have glimpses through Scripture about what comes after death. "Your word is a lamp for my feet, a light on my path" (Psalm 119:105). Some of these passages may be a comfort to the older people you love. As we enter the last season of life, we are invited to engage with these living words, to find the light for the journey, even to death.

1. JESUS TELLS US ABOUT LIFE AFTER DEATH

Jesus said to her, "I am the resurrection and the life. The one who believes in me will live, even though they die."

JOHN 11:25

"Very truly I tell you, whoever hears my word and believes him who sent me has eternal life and will not be judged but has crossed over from death to life."

JOHN 5:24

"Do not let your hearts be troubled. You believe in God; believe also in me. My Father's house has many rooms; if that were not so, would I have told you that I am going there to prepare a place for you? And if I go and prepare a place for you, I will come back and take you to be with me that you also may be where I am."

JOHN 14:1-3

Pick one of these verses to reflect on. What, in particular, comforts you today?

2. THE PSALMIST SPEAKS OF REST

Therefore my heart is glad, and my soul
rejoices; my body also rests secure.

PSALM 16:9, NRSV

What invitation from God do you hear in this verse?

3. PAUL REMINDS US WE WILL NEVER BE SEPARATED FROM GOD

I am convinced that neither death nor life,
neither angels nor demons, neither the
present nor the future, nor any powers,
neither height nor depth, nor anything else
in all creation, will be able to separate us
from the love of God that is in Christ Jesus
our Lord.

ROMANS 8:38-39

*What similar words would you use to describe your
own life?*

4. THE REVELATION OF JOHN REVEALS WHAT WE CAN EXPECT AFTER DEATH

Whoever has ears, let them hear what the Spirit says to the churches. To the one who is victorious, I will give some of the hidden manna. I will also give that person a white stone with a new name written on it, known only to the one who receives it.

REVELATION 2:17

He will wipe every tear from their eyes. There will be no more death or mourning or crying or pain, for the old order of things has passed away.

REVELATION 21:4

What would you like your new name to be?

What parts of your life are you hoping will be part of the "old order of things" that have passed away? How would you like to be waiting for that to happen?

Appendix 2

One Man's Perspective on Aging Faithfully

My husband, Bob, and I entered the aging process at about the same time. But it looked different for both of us. Bob was retiring from a job and was looking for ways to continue to use his gifts. I was retiring from life as I had known it. I was looking for ways to use my gifts in quieter, less public ways. Even though I walked beside Bob through his retirement, I decided to ask him some questions about what his journey looks like even as he continues in this new season of life.

WHAT FEELINGS DID YOU HAVE AS YOU ANTICIPATED RETIREMENT?

I looked forward to the relief of relinquishing many of the responsibilities of my leadership role. I was eager to let go of budgets, planning, and the need to keep moving the company forward. As much as I liked the opportunity to lead, mentor, and supervise others, I looked forward to letting go of performance appraisals and salary administration. I was eager for more personal freedom with my time, more time to rest, and more time to be with family.

Amid the early months of anticipation, I also felt deep sadness. I did not want to lose my long-term professional relationships or the daily connections with office colleagues. I also knew I would be losing some of my identity as a Christian leader and the opportunities to use the gifts God has given me. For fifty years, I had been in positions of leadership in Christian organizations. It was hard to think of life without the recognition and experiences those positions gave. And it was a surprise to me that I did not want to lose my expense account! I had subconsciously found indications of worth from the perks of the job.

HOW DID YOU RESPOND TO THE GIFTS AND LOSSES OF THIS NEW SEASON? WHAT DID YOU CELEBRATE, AND HOW DID YOU GRIEVE?

I definitely celebrated the blessedness of not having to be responsible for so much. I celebrated the time to be available to my family when they needed me rather than when I scheduled them in. I am growing in my appreciation for relationships and learning to be attentive to others outside of any professional connections.

My own losses were not so much physical, although I have slowed down a bit. The losses I feel most deeply are the personal and professional losses and how these affect my view of myself. These are the parts of retirement I grieve the most.

In the years before I retired, I took several four-day retreats at a friend's home on Lake Michigan. I was alone with a lot of time to reflect on my vocational years, remember the good and the bad, and begin letting go—a little more with each retreat. Those days were very helpful to me, both in grief and in moving forward.

As I moved closer to retirement, I asked four friends to meet with Alice and me for a "clearness committee." This is a Quaker practice of gathering a small group of people to help with discernment. Meeting with our friends gave clarity about how to navigate the timing of my retirement as well as perspectives on the many questions that would follow that decision.

Another thing that helped me with both celebrating and grieving was deep, personal engagement with Scripture. On one retreat, I spent time in Ezekiel 47:1-12. I felt like I went along with Ezekiel as he experienced his vision of the temple. He saw a flowing stream and trees along the bank of the river. Ezekiel also saw stagnant water, but as the water from the Temple flowed into the sea, the water there became fresh. God said to the prophet, "Son of man, do you see this?" (Ezekiel 47:6). I felt as though God said to me, "Bob, do you see this?" I hoped that my life in retirement would be a river like that. As I read those verses, I knew that whatever I did in retirement, I wanted to be part of the healing streams of water, to no longer feel responsible for planting the trees and "organizing" the water. "Where the river flows everything will live" (Ezekiel 47:9). I hoped, by God's grace, that this would describe my life. Ezekiel's vision continues to speak to me.

HOW HAS YOUR RETIREMENT (AND THE PROCESS OF AGING) CHANGED YOUR RELATIONSHIP WITH GOD?

By God's grace, I am letting go of my need for recognition. I am learning to be content with the life I have now. I try to remember to celebrate with gratitude all the blessings of my life. God has invited me, with a spiritual play on words, to be living in the presence of God in the present moment and to be a present to others. It is quite a transition for me to move from a life of public ministry to helping out with driving my granddaughter to school. I am surprised at the joy that is bringing into my life.

Appendix 3

The Bridge between Generations

GROWING OLDER is not a solo experience. No matter our marital status, the number of living relatives we have, where we live, or how old we are, we will likely experience the aging process in communities. For most of us, our community includes those younger and older than we are. Some of our communities include our own parents as well as our adult children. Those who are single probably have extended families and a circle of friends, also of a variety of ages. I asked a number of my own friends to respond to questions about how they would like others to help them as they experience getting older. Specifically, I asked my older friends about what they would like their children to know about them in their senior years. I asked my midlife friends about what they would like their senior parents to know about their own view of life and family as their parents are aging. And I asked my single friends about what they would like their married friends to know about what it is like to be single as they grow older. When my friends responded to my questions, I was able to glean insights that offer us a bridge between generations as we continue the ongoing experience of being faithful to God and to others as we age.

OLDER PARENTS WITH ADULT CHILDREN

The main question I asked my older friends was: *What would you like your children to know about you in your senior years?* Several answers kept showing up in my inbox.

1. Parents want their children to know how much they love them.

One friend said that she and her husband wanted their children to know "that they are the most important people in our lives."

Another friend said, "I want them to know how much I appreciate and love them and really value them and how they have led their lives. My admiration for each of them is very deep, and I want them to know that."

2. Older parents want to stay connected with their adult children.

"The most important contribution they can make to our well-being is staying in touch with us. Visits are great when they are possible, but frequent phone conversations about their lives, activities, and issues, and those of their kids, are a close runner-up."

One of my friends was honest enough to mention that ways of communication are different for our children. "Phone calls, visits, do I even dare to dream of an email or a letter these days? It is very dissatisfying to settle for text messaging, which we can hardly get them to answer anyway."

Another friend noticed that as he and his wife have aged, he senses that "our ignoring things like Instagram or TikTok may look to them like we're in the Dark Ages."

3. Older parents hope their children will accept them as their physical energy diminishes.

"My limitations are increasing. I cannot do life in the same manner as in younger years."

"Taking care of myself requires more time and attention as I age."

"My energy tank is smaller, but I'm no longer driven to accomplish. Intensity does not energize me."

4. My friends hope for more than a passing nod from their children.

"I've grown accustomed to frequent losses, leaving a thin layer of accumulated grief. Sometimes I need to feel that or talk about family that have gone."

"I love having time and adult conversation without the grandchildren."

"Our children tend to have little interest in the mementos and photos that help us relive family times and significant events. What do you do with all the diplomas, plaques, trophies, and bronzed baby shoes?" She concluded, "The answer is simple (to let go), but it is not easy."

"Even if we donate our stuff to Goodwill, we would still like to talk about the events behind the stuff! In fact, we like to talk with our kids about almost anything."

5. Parents want their children to know that they are still changing, even as they age.

"I keep growing. In many ways, I'm not the same person they remember when they were living under our roof. My spiritual life and views have grown exponentially beyond where I was when they were younger."

"I would like my children to know that although my core values remain much the same, the edges have softened."

"I want them to see me as I am. To acknowledge that I've changed and am still changing."

6. Older parents do not want to be intrusive in their children's lives but have questions about how to do that.

"I relish learning real things about their lives but I am wary of being too intrusive."

"Sometimes expressing my opinions feels either unnecessary or presumptuous."

"My son juggles a lot of relational and professional demands on his time and energy. I don't want to ask much of him in this life chapter."

"I don't have the same physical energy I used to, but I have a lot to offer in terms of wisdom."

7. It is hard to talk about end-of-life issues.

"It's not too early to begin to have much more detailed conversations about these things with the kids: If I die first, my wife will need help with the finances. If she dies first, I will need help with household activities. If our minds begin to go, we will need help caring for each other and sorting out what that care looks like." This friend acknowledged that these are not easy topics to bring up with their children.

"I hope that our children will have adequate resources (desire, time, and energy) to be mindful and attentive to our changing/increasing needs."

"We hope to have a conversation (or two) about potential changes before they feel they need to insist."

"I would like them to ask us about any changes in our desires for the future and end of life."

"We hope they will be attentive, communicate perhaps even more frequently, and notice when we need more help."

"Feel free to give us feedback or make suggestions. But trust us to have the capacity to make wise decisions too."

"I fully plan on being creative, positive, and courageous while aging. I hope my children will be kind when this is a struggle for me."

ADULT CHILDREN WATCHING THEIR PARENTS AGE

Along with my emails to my senior friends, I emailed questions to midlife friends about what it was like to watch their parents age. Their answers gave me additional insights about the bridge between older parents and their children.

1. Just as my older friends wanted their children to know how much they loved them, many of my younger friends wanted their parents to know how much they appreciated them.

"My parents have died, and I don't remember telling them how the good qualities people saw in me came from them. I wish I could thank them for the solid life foundation they provided: the largely unconditional love, the values they modeled, the rich spiritual heritage, the relational and emotional maturity."

"I wouldn't be who I am personally or professionally without them."

"I love my parents! I'm so proud of them and inspired by them!"

2. Some adult children had regrets.

"My parents raised us to be not very close as a family, and they still repeat that as our family mode of operating. It is disappointing. It is not a model I like. It is hard to overcome. And I think they missed out on relationship with their children and grandchildren. They are still keeping us at arms' length."

3. Adult children are sad to see the physical diminishment of their parents.

"As I watch my parents age, I mourn with them the things they can no longer do the way they did before."

"I also find that I have a lot of fear about their health and safety. When they go to the doctor, I find myself anxious to hear if the doctor had any concerns."

"They lack the energy and stamina to do the things they used to do and are very frustrated by that. They still have the desire to do it all. I don't know how to be helpful without making them feel condescended to. Conversely, sometimes I don't help when I should, which I think is unintentionally hurtful. It's hard to navigate our new roles."

"It's hard to watch them be tired more. It's hard on them, but it's hard on us to watch, too, as we contemplate what that signals."

"I don't like watching my mother's body grow weak."

"I find myself trying to figure out if they're okay or what might be giving them trouble because I don't trust them to tell me."

4. Children notice that their parents have changed.

"My parents have each mellowed and live with less stress than I remember from the past."

"Mom had always struggled with a poor self-image. Somehow in the last month of her life, she was finally able to take in her identity as a beloved child of God. So freeing, so life-giving, so wonderful!"

"We relate to one another in more even-keeled ways. Relating to them feels more person-to-person than adult-to-child or senior-to-junior."

"My parents seem much more relaxed around their grandchildren compared to how they were when we were growing up."

5. Adult children wish their parents accepted them in the areas where they disagree.

"I wish my parents understood that it is okay for me to have different opinions than they do. I want them to know that they don't need to feel threatened by or fearful of my opinions that differ from theirs."

"At the moment, my parents seem to think I am going through a 'phase' (a shift in faith belief) and will eventually come back around. I wish they understood it's probably not a phase but a new stage. It would be easier to discuss with them. Instead I tend to avoid talking about it much. It just feels more respectful, but it creates a distance that I wish wasn't there."

6. Adult children want their parents to know that they are doing well.

"I wish I could tell [my mother] that we're all going to be okay. We'll have our regrets, our experiences, our successes, our tragedies, and we'll all be okay in the end, in part because our parents were so good to all of us."

"My mother is the best in me."

FACING AGING AS A SINGLE PERSON

I also asked my single friends about their experiences of aging. I especially wanted to hear what they would like their married friends to know about what it is like to get older as a single person. Their answers were varied and included perspectives that also apply to younger single people. As with much in the process of aging, these familiar experiences take on a new intensity as we age.

1. Several of my single friends pointed out that aging as a single person is not that different, spiritually and physically, from aging as a married person.

One friend said, "I think aging affects people fairly similarly, regardless of marital status. More aches and less agility, maybe a little slower thinking process, and maybe changes in what is of interest to you." Then she made this insightful observation: "It seems that people either get better and better (more kind, thoughtful, settled) or more bitter as they age. And that all happens whether you are single or married."

Another friend said, "In terms of spiritual formation, I am not sure that things are too different between married people and singles." She went on to say that the biggest differences she has noticed are the practical ones: "Who will take care of me? Who will I leave my things to? How can I figure out Medicare?"

2. Practical issues came up again and again. Most of these issues involved medical care and financial complications.

One friend wrote, "When I watch a married friend support a sick spouse, I can find myself wondering, *Who will do that for me?*"

Another friend said, "I am less naive about the likelihood that I will need help in practical ways in the years to come. Without children or a spouse, I feel more responsible to plan as best I can for possible health issues in the decades ahead. I am old enough now to feel some growing vulnerability as a single aging adult. I will not have children who can play a role in making health decisions, should I be unable to do this."

"I am single, never married, and that means I have a single-income household. At times, this can feel limiting in how and where I live. It also can affect things like level of insurance and preparing for retirement. I may need to work later into life than my married friends, especially if they are/were a two-income family. Sometimes I feel alone in facing all of this."

3. My single friends asked for understanding, acceptance, and inclusion from their married friends.

"As someone who is single with married friends, I want them to know that being included in their families is a wonderful thing."

"Most of my same-aged friends have kids and grandkids, so those are the common topics when we get together. I love hearing about their worlds, but often my world isn't all that interesting to them. My stories may not be like theirs, but I do have stories to tell. Ask me about where I've seen God provide for me, take care of me, or show up and do what only he could have done. Inquire about the highlights and challenges I've faced in life. I have lots of stories I can tell if you'll express interest."

"I have some dear friends who have families and who always invite me to join them when it comes to holidays and just doing life. They are not trying to fix me or keep me busy, but they are always open to me joining them, and if they don't invite me over, I can just invite myself."

"Being alone is harder as I get older. I yearn for someone to share/do life with. It means a lot when married friends can get out and take time as individuals and not just as a couple. One-on-one time is important."

4. Another frequent response to my questions for my single friends has to do with an attitude toward singleness that they felt from their married friends.

"You don't need to feel pity or sadness for me. Many single people may struggle emotionally with growing older as a single person, but don't assume that all single people lament their single state. If you are not sure how it is for your single friends, just ask them how it feels to be single before voicing your condolences. It feels much better to be listened to than to have someone try to fix something that may not be broken."

"I think one of the hurtful things married people do is to assume all people are like them. Statements like, 'Well, we all know that because we've learned it raising children' may communicate that there is no other way God will teach us."

5. My single friends, especially the women, appreciate practical help from their married friends.

"If they are able, I appreciate my married friends doing practical things for me to help. But if I ask for help, it feels tough when someone responds in ways that make me feel like a burden to them. I love it when someone communicates, 'I'm on it!' No questions asked."

"Big decisions are one of the hardest things for me as a single because I'm having to make those decisions all alone. Having married friends who are willing to walk alongside me when those decisions and challenges come along is very helpful."

6. Single people may experience problems in church at any age. My older single friends indicated that this is still difficult for them.

"Church is very married-centric. As a single woman, I often feel invisible in church. This isn't just an age-oriented challenge, but it is exacerbated by aging. . . . So much of ministry is geared toward men, and women's ministry is geared toward moms and stay-at-home wives. More often than not, the women's groups meet during the day, which doesn't fit for those of us who work. And often, the studies are geared toward marriage and raising kids. It can feel rather unwelcoming when there is rarely a time spot and a topic that fits my realities."

"During the pandemic, my small group met by Zoom. After some discussion about pandemic-related issues, the leader summarized by saying, 'Well, it sounds like we all find the best thing for us is having someone we live with that we can enjoy.' That is not true for me, and it was hurtful."

7. Most of my friends have a healthy, proactive attitude about aging as a single person.

"One thing that comes up among some of my single women friends is financial need. . . . We try to help one another financially as we can and as we are aware of needs."

"Several of my friends in their nineties don't want to leave their houses and go into care homes. I think we need to think about future arrangements well before our nineties! I have a loving sister and family, but I don't want to be a burden to them if I live to that great age."

"As a single, I've found that aging can be delightful, even if difficult at times. I have fewer things tying me down, and I can choose to travel more or be spontaneous with my time in ways that my married friends are not able to do. As I age, I find that I know what I am good at and I can leverage that for God's Kingdom quite differently than I used to when I was still trying to discover who I am."

Notes

INTRODUCTION

1. Zalman Schachter-Shalomi and Ronald S. Miller, *From Age-ing to Sage-ing: A Profound New Vision of Growing Older* (New York: Warner Books, 1997), 23–24.

CHAPTER 1: A DIFFERENT KIND OF RETIREMENT

1. For more commentary on what Jesus meant, see https://biblehub .com/commentaries/luke/5-37.htm.

CHAPTER 2: EXPERIENCING NEW BIRTH AS WE AGE

1. David Benner, *The Gift of Being Yourself: The Sacred Call to Self-Discovery* (Downers Grove, IL: InterVarsity Press, 2015), 72.

CHAPTER 3: HOLY LOSSES, HOLY INVITATIONS

1. Zalman Schachter-Shalomi and Ronald S. Miller, *From Age-ing to Sage-ing: A Profound New Vision of Growing Older* (New York: Warner Books, 1997), 17, 19.
2. David Brooks, "The Wisdom Your Body Knows: You Are Not Just Thinking with Your Brain," *New York Times*, November 28, 2019, https://www.nytimes.com/2019/11/28/opinion/brain-body -thinking.html.

3. "The Gut-Brain Connection," Harvard Health Publishing, updated January 21, 2020, https://www.health.harvard.edu/diseases-and-conditions/the-gut-brain-connection.

4. Bill Simpson, "Aging for Amateurs: Taking Care of Our Vagus Nerves," *Post and Courier*, updated September 14, 2020, https://www.postandcourier.com/columnists/aging-for-amateurs-taking-care-of-our-vagus-nerves/article_a8147ed4-3a9d-11e9-a3ba-ef05d1db0b08.html.

5. Kirstin Butler, "This Is Your Body on Music," Medium, July 14, 2016, https://medium.com/the-sound-of-innovation/this-is-your-body-on-music-3c4d65d5b113.

CHAPTER 4: LETTING GO

1. John Calvin, quoted in Carolyn Nystrom, *John Calvin: Sovereign Hope*, Christian Classics Bible Studies (Downers Grove, IL: InterVarsity Press, 2002), 13–14.

2. Parker Palmer, *On the Brink of Everything: Grace, Gravity and Getting Old* (Oakland, CA: Berrett–Koehler, 2018), 8.

3. Thomas H. Green, *Weeds Among the Wheat: Discernment: Where Prayer and Action Meet* (Notre Dame: Ave Maria Press, 1984), 22.

4. Adele Ahlberg Calhoun, *Spiritual Disciplines Handbook: Practices that Transform Us* (Downers Grove, IL: InterVarsity Press, 2005), 53–55.

5. Green, *Weeds among the Wheat*, 145.

6. Phileena Heuertz, *Mindful Silence: The Heart of Christian Contemplation* (Downers Grove, IL: InterVarsity Press, 2018), 62.

CHAPTER 5: FEAR AND PEACE

1. Parker Palmer, *On the Brink of Everything: Grace, Gravity and Getting Old* (Oakland, CA: Berrett-Koehler, 2018), 176. Emphasis in original.

2. Richard Rohr's Daily Meditation, The Center for Action and Contemplation, April 5, 2020, https://cac.org/five-consoling-messages-2020-04-05/.

3. David Steindl-Rast, *Gratefulness, the Heart of Prayer: An Approach to Life in Fullness* (Mahwah, NJ: Paulist Press, 1984), 212.

4. *Pascal's Pensées*, trans. W. F. Trotter (New York: E. P. Dutton, 1958), 39.

5. Etty Hillesum, *An Interrupted Life: The Diaries, 1941–1943* and *Letters from Westerbork* (New York: Owl Books, 1996), 218.

EPILOGUE: LISTENING WELL TO AGING FRIENDS

1. Curt Thompson, *Anatomy of the Soul: Surprising Connections between Neuroscience and Spiritual Practices That Can Transform Your Life and Relationships* (Carol Stream, IL: SaltRiver, 2010), 3.

2. Thompson, *Anatomy of the Soul*, 3.

3. Atul Gawande, *Being Mortal: Medicine and What Matters in the End* (New York: Metropolitan Books, 2014), 177–78.

4. Gawande, *Being Mortal*, 212–13.

About the Author

ALICE FRYLING is a spiritual director and author. Her books on relationships, spiritual formation, and spiritual direction have sold over half a million copies and are published in over ten languages. She and her husband, Bob, are parents of two daughters and grandparents of two grandsons and two granddaughters. They live in Monument, Colorado. Learn more about Alice at www.alicefryling.com.

THE NAVIGATORS® STORY

T HANK YOU for picking up this NavPress book! We hope it has been a blessing to you.

NavPress is a ministry of The Navigators. The Navigators began in the 1930s, when a young California lumberyard worker named Dawson Trotman was impacted by basic discipleship principles and felt called to teach those principles to others. He saw this mission as an echo of 2 Timothy 2:2: "And the things you have heard me say in the presence of many witnesses entrust to reliable people who will also be qualified to teach others" (NIV).

In 1933, Trotman and his friends began discipling members of the US Navy. By the end of World War II, thousands of men on ships and bases around the world were learning the principles of spiritual multiplication by the intentional, person-to-person teaching of God's Word.

After World War II, The Navigators expanded its relational ministry to include college campuses; local churches; the Glen Eyrie Conference Center and Eagle Lake Camps in Colorado Springs, Colorado; and neighborhood and citywide initiatives across the country and around the world.

Today, with more than 2,600 US staff members—and local ministries in more than 100 countries—The Navigators continues the transformational process of making disciples who make more disciples, advancing the Kingdom of God in a world that desperately needs the hope and salvation of Jesus Christ and the encouragement to grow deeper in relationship with Him.

NAVPRESS was created in 1975 to advance the calling of The Navigators by bringing biblically rooted and culturally relevant products to people who want to know and love Christ more deeply. In January 2014, NavPress entered an alliance with Tyndale House Publishers to strengthen and better position our rich content for the future. Through *THE MESSAGE* Bible and other resources, NavPress seeks to bring positive spiritual movement to people's lives.

If you're interested in learning more or becoming involved with The Navigators, go to navigators.org. For more discipleship content from The Navigators and NavPress authors, visit thedisciplemaker.org. May God bless you in your walk with Him!

navpress.com

CP1308